FOODIE'S BEER BOOK

THE FOODIE'S BEER BOOK

THE ART OF PAIRING AND COOKING WITH BEER FOR ANY OCCASION

BROOKE AND **LUTHER FEDORA**

Skyhorse Publishing

Skyhorse Publishing books may be purchased in bulk at special discounts for sales promotion, corporate gifts, fund-raising, or educational purposes. Special editions can also be created to specifications. For details, contact the Special Sales Department, Skyhorse Publishing, 307 West 36th Street, 11th Floor, New York, NY 10018 or info@skyhorsepublishing.com.

Skyhorse® and Skyhorse Publishing® are registered trademarks of Skyhorse Publishing, Inc. ®, a Delaware corporation.

www.skyhorsepublishing.com

10 9 8 7 6 5 4 3 2 1

Library of Congress Cataloging-in-Publication Data is available on file.

ISBN: 978-1-62873-682-3
Ebook ISBN: 978-1-62914-108-4

Printed in China

CONTENTS

SPRING

SUMMER

AUTUMN

Luther Fedora

INTRODUCTION

Luther and I are so pleased to have the opportunity to compile our favorite recipes and beer dinner menus for this book. This project was born out of our love for both specialty beer and food. Our cooking has been greatly enhanced by the unique flavors that beer and food create when paired together.

Our story began in 2007 when we had the great pleasure of opening our first restaurant in Charlottesville, Virginia. The Horse & Hound Gastropub is a casual eatery that specializes in great beer from around the world, local wine, and simple food made with fresh ingredients and lots of love.

At the Culinary Institute of America, we were educated in the art of cooking with wine, and learned the intricacies of melding and concentrating the various flavors of reds and whites into our food. But it was not until we opened the Horse and Hound Gastropub that our education in the art of cooking with beer really began. With a wealth of beers at our disposal, we started to experiment, first with rich sauces and delicate marinades, then with complex soups, light batters, and eventually stunning and surprising desserts. Soon five-course beer dinners replaced the standard wine dinners, and started the celebration of beer as an integral ingredient in our restaurant's menu.

Of course, cooking with beer was not a completely novel experience to us. My first introduction to cooking with beer was my grandmother's Welsh rarebit. It was just a simple sauce made of beer and sharp Wisconsin cheddar, poured over toasted rye bread. I watched as she poured the dark beer into the pot, seeing its bubbles hit the hot sauce and scamper across the surface before being whisked into the whole. Although I know she thought of it as the simplest of dinners, it seemed to me the most exotic of dishes. Over the years, I watched as my grandpa threw a bottle of beer into his chili, or a can was "shared" with the barbecued ribs on the grill. "Beer can chicken" was a staple on Sunday afternoons.

The beautiful beers of Europe inspired our palates, but the art of beer making has reached into every region of America. Micro-breweries and home brewers are creating magical concoctions, and even the larger breweries are beginning to appreciate the artful touch of a well-crafted small batch beer. Fruits, spices, and smoking techniques have broadened the array of flavors past the traditional hops and malts. We have had the unique opportunity to travel the world through beer. We have discovered the sweet, balanced flavors of Belgium, the intense hops from California, the mild ambers of the UK, and the dry ciders from France. Beer has been a staple in every culture and continues to unite us all around the dinner table.

This book is a compilation of some of our favorite beer dinners. Whether you are feeding a football crowd or creating a full-blown dinner party, there is something in here that will please and surprise every palate. And don't stop at our recipes! Once you understand the basic flavors that beer imparts, let your imagination loose and adapt our recipes to your own favorite brews! Cheers!

Brooke and Luther Fedora
Charlottesville, Virginia

BEER—A BRIEF HISTORY

It would not be surprising if our ancient ancestors considered beer a "gift from the gods." In all likelihood that first batch of homebrew was a happy accident—the result of grains fermenting spontaneously after interacting with wild yeast in the air. However that first batch occurred, it wasn't long before batches were being brewed on purpose. Records show grain-based beer being made in Mesopotamia where it was often used medicinally or in religious ceremonies.

An understanding of brew culture spread throughout the grain-growing cultures. Soon a number of variations appeared, relying on the variety of wild yeasts and grains that were readily available. The early beers were not strained, creating a porridge-like sludge that was consumed from shallow bowls. Beer gained popularity in regions where grapes did not flourish. Not only did it provide a ready supply of calories for the working class population, it was a healthful alternative to the unsanitary water that would have been available to the masses.

Because early beer did not travel well, brewing was generally a home-based activity. Herbs were often added for flavor, and it was discovered that the addition of hops, a small bitter flowering plant, helped to preserve the beer. The addition of hops allowed beer to be exported. Some may have turned up their noses at the bitter brew, preferring the purer ales that relied solely on the combination of water, malt, and yeast. But that distinctive hoppy taste soon became emblematic of true beer.

HOW BEER IS MADE

Before we get started cooking with beer, it makes sense to understand exactly what beer is, and the best way to do that is to make a batch yourself! All beer is made up of a handful of simple ingredients—grains, hops, yeast and water. It is the combination of those ingredients where the magic lies.

MALTED GRAIN

Grain that has been processed to produce enzymes for the conversion of the grain's starch into fermentable sugars is called malt. Grains processed this way provide the food that the yeast will need to develop alcohol and carbon dioxide. Barley is the traditional grain of choice for malt but other grains, such as wheat, rice, oats, and corn can also be used. The malt is steeped into a kind of tea called a wort, and used as the base for the beer. Malt provides sweet, caramel, toasted flavors to the bitter and adds body to the brew.

HOPS

The flower of the hops vine is called hops, and is the primary flavoring for beer. Where malt provides the engine and the sweet body of the beer, it is the hops that provides much of the traditional character one thinks of in a traditional beer. The hops contribute a distinctive bitterness, along with hints of citrus, floral, piney, and herbal notes. Hops is also responsible for the beer's distinctive "head."

YEAST

The yeast pulls everything together, eating up the sugar from the grain and converting the blend into bubbly goodness. There are two primary yeast types: top-fermenting yeast which is used to make ales, and bottom-fermenting yeasts which are used to make lager styles. The two yeast types, each with different temperature environments and aging times, produce beers with decidedly different characteristics. Most yeast these days are commercially produced although "wild" or airborne yeasts are sometimes used by purists.

WATER

When it comes to beer, it's not "just" water. As you may remember from the beer commercials with flowing mountain streams, the quality and type of water can be an important component of the beer-making process. Brewers have found that the presence of a high sulfate content in water results in a sharp, clean bitterness while water high in carbonates creates a harsh, clinging bitterness. Hard water produces a different beer than softer water, and minerals present in natural spring waters can also add to a beer's natural body and effervescence.

LUTHER'S BEER RECIPE

We rely heavily on the wealth of beer styles and flavors from the world's breweries. But with all the different types available, what self-respecting chef wouldn't want to make his own? Here is Luther's favorite recipe.

Belgian Tripel- ABV 8.5-9%
Makes a 5 gallon batch
4 ounces Belgian Aromatic grains
6.6 pounds light liquid malt extract
3 pounds Pilsen dried malt extract
1 pound light candi sugar
8 ounces Maltodextrin
1 ounce Northern Brewer hops
1/2 ounce UK Golding hops
1 pint starter abbey ale yeast WLP530

In a 4 gallon stock pot bring 2 1/2 gallons of water to about 150–165 degrees. Place the aromatic grains in a grain bag and steep in the hot water for 20 minutes. Remove the grain bag and let it drain without squeezing it. Your water is now wort. Bring your wort to a boil and add the liquid malt extract, dried malt extract, maltodextrin, and

candi sugar, stirring constantly, return to a rolling boil. Add the Northern Brewer hops and boil for 50 minutes, after this time add the UK Golding hops and boil for 5 minutes. Remove from the heat. Cool the wort to about 70 degrees. When cool, pour the wort into a sanitized fermenter, do not transfer the sediment from the pot. Add about 2 ½ gallons of water at about 70 degrees to the wort, the mix should measure 5 gallons total. Sprinkle the

yeast over the wort and stir until combined. Secure the lid on your fermenter with an airlock. Store the wort in a dark, warm space with a controlled temperature of about 64–72 degrees. Fermentation begins and will last about 1 week. Bottle and store in a temperature stable space about 64–72 degrees for about 2 weeks. Chill and enjoy.

CHARACTERISTICS OF BEER

APPEARANCE

Beer color is dictated by the reaction of the enzymes to the sugars in the beer. The color is measured in Lovibond degrees, which range from a pale lager at 2 degrees and any Imperial stout ranging up to 40 or more. Color usually comes from the malt, with roasted malt creating a darker color and richer flavor. Clarity is a factor of both color and ingredients; a light hefeweizen may be somewhat cloudy because of the presence of yeast while a thick malty stout may be almost impossible to see through. Beer is also described as thin, thick, or even creamy, all ways to describe the relative viscosity and body of the beer. The beer's head is also a factor of beer type. A wheat beer tends to have a bigger, longer lasting head, while some darker beers have just a skim of foam.

STRENGTH

There are a number of factors that go into beer strength. The amount of malt, the variety of yeast, and the metabolism of sugars all play a role. Beers brewed at cooler temperatures or for shorter periods tend to be lower in alcohol content. Balancing all these factors is the key to producing both flavor and punch. Beers typically range from about 3% alcohol by volume to over 14%.

EFFERVESCENCE

It's all about the bubbles. When the sugars finish metabolizing into carbon dioxide, effervescence occurs. Lighter beers tend to have larger bubbles. This effervescence makes it a great ingredient for fish and onion ring batters because the bubbles help to create a lighter crust.

AROMA AND FLAVOR

Like wine, beer comes with an array of terms that attempt to describe its aroma and flavor. The most common terms refer to its ingredients. A beer that is "hoppy" is spicier, bitter, or citrusy. A "malty" flavor tastes grainy or caramelized. Light beers may be considered fruity or floral or crisp. Darker beers are often labeled robust, roasted, or buttery.

BEER TYPES

It hardly seems possible given all the beers we have available today, but traditional beer falls into two basic categories: Ale and Lager.

ALE

The original "ale" recipes did not allow for anything but malt and yeast to be combined with water. But over time, the word "ale" tended to refer to any strong beer. Today, ales are defined by the type of yeast that is used in brewing. Ale yeasts clump together, (known as flocculating) at the top of the fermentation tank, in room temperature conditions of 60–70 degrees. After fermentation, ales are aged at 40–55 degrees, generally for just a few weeks. This method creates a round, complex beer that has a rich aroma and big flavor. Ales are often served at room temperature or just slightly chilled.

The following beers all fall into the ale category.

WHEAT BEER

Wheat beers are typically brewed with 30–70% wheat malt. Because wheat contains a lot more protein than barley, the wheat protein create a creamy mouthfeel. a thick, long-lasting head and a somewhat hazy appearance. You can easily recognize wheat beer by its name, although that name is not often "wheat." Look for "weiz," "weizen," or "wit" to identify wheat beers.

The most well know of wheat beers is the hefeweizen, which is an unfiltered wheat ale that often tastes of banana, cloves, and light citrus. These beers are light and easy to drink on a hot summer day, and are perfect paired with a wedge of orange or lemon. The Belgium witbier is brewed in a similar fashion to the hefeweizen but with a different strain of yeast, often with the addition of orange peel and coriander.

Berliner Weisse, first brewed in Northern Germany, is fermented with ale yeast and Lactobacillus Delbruckii. This creates a unique, sour flavor for which Berliner Weisse is famous.

Because wheat provides a lot of texture but little flavor to the beer, it is a popular ingredient in fruit beers. A good example of a fruit beer made with wheat is Fruli by Brouwerij Huyghe from Belgium, this beer is a blend of 70% wheat and 30% fruit juice.

The malty darker wheat beers, such as Dunkelweizen and Weizenbock are made in a similar fashion as the lighter hefeweizens but use a heartier malt variety like Vienna or Munich malts. These rich nutty flavors added to the typical hefeweizen flavor of cloves and bananas really creates a nicely balanced yet complex beer. Pair pale wheat beer with light dishes like salad and fish. Seek out the darker version to go with grilled steak or heartier stews.

BITTER

Because a traditional bitter has very little carbonation, it is always served on tap. Technically, once it is bottled, it would be considered a pale ale. But you will certainly see that rule broken. Bitters are best served quite cold, and are perfect with fatty meats and greasy bacon and eggs.

PALE ALE

The pale ale category is pretty large and cannot be nailed down to just your traditional pale style of beer. The beers in this category are known as lighter, easy-to-drink beers which are generally lower in alcohol than other brews. This category is commonly thought of as traditional English Pale Ale, and includes bitters and ESBs, otherwise know as Extra Special (or Strong) Bitter. British pale ales tend to be well balanced, with malty, wood, and slight floral hop characteristics.

The American versions of pale ales tend to be more aggressively hopped, lending them a slightly spicy flavor profile. American Pale Ale typically consists of cascade hops which adds more bitterness, bringing this beer to just below a typical IPA in flavor. These are typically around 5% ABV. Amber Ales are brewed with crystal malts which add an amber color and slightly maltier flavor. Irish Red Ale is darker—an amber-red color with malty undertones.

Strong Ale is another pale ale that has been amped up. This variety is made with pale malts and ranges in strength from 5% ABV to as much as 41% ABV, although a typical strong ale is around 7–8% ABV.

Scotch Ale is similar to strong ale, but tends towards sweetness and fuller body. Blonde Ales are very pale in color with a clear, crisp, and dry flavor. They tend to have a low to medium bitterness and balanced, low alcohol beers.

One of our favorite Blonde Ales is Duvel from Belgium. Biere de Garde is a traditional French pale ale that is sometimes referred to as "farmhouse ale" that are bottled and aged.

Pale ales are universally pleasing and can be served with a wide range of foods. When choosing one for your meal, consider one with malty undertones for caramelized, sweet, and roasted flavors. Use more bitter versions to cut through fat, and balanced blondes for lighter fare, like salad and green vegetables.

INDIAN PALE ALES AND IMPERIAL IPA

While IPA was created to solve a problem, it wasn't long before its crisp, hoppy taste became popular across the world. In the 18th and 19th centuries, the British found themselves struggling to ship beer to their counterparts in India. The traditional sweet, malty ales just weren't stable enough to withstand such long journeys, and often arrived spoiled and sour. In the 1790s the Bow Brewery in London tried adding lots of extra hops, grains, and sugar to their original pale ale recipe. These additions created a stronger beer in both flavor, and alcohol and hop bitterness, resulting in a more stable beer. This innovation quickly made them the leading exporters of IPAs, and making them the brewing capital of England.

Today, IPA is among the best selling, most popular variety of beer. English IPAs are mild and balanced, while the American IPAs of the East Coast are also less hopped and tend to have a more balance, malty favor. On the West Coast, IPAs tend to be bigger, with bold and heavily hopped notes with little evidence of malt. Imperial IPAs are amped-up IPA. They are higher in alcohol and tend to have strong citrus or pine notes balanced with a malt backbone.

IPAs pair well with citrus desserts, salads, and grilled meats. Because of their bitter hoppiness, they don't do well in stews or simmered dishes.

LAGER

Unlike ales, which are produced with top-fermenting yeasts, the yeasts used to make lager clump together close to the bottom of the tank. Lagers prefer cooler conditions in the tank of 45–55 degrees.

Because lager yeasts are aggressive fermenters, they leave behind little residual sweetness. Aging is often done for several months, in temperatures at least ten degrees cooler than traditional ales. The result is a crisp, clean refreshing beer with less aroma and flavor. Lagers are typically 3–5% ABV and are best served cold.

The very first lagers were brewed in Germany. They were dark lagers called Dunkels and are still produced today. They are dark, heavily hopped and malted lagers. Other types of Lagers are the Bock, Doppledock, and Eisbock. These beers are all related; they build from the base Bock, a strong, dark lager that pours clear copper in color and has an ABV of 6.3–7.2%.

Bocks are rich and toasty with caramel notes. The Doppledock is a stronger version of the Bock, dark brown in color with ABVs ranging from 7–12%. They taste rich and malty with hints of chocolate and some fruitiness. The Eisbock is made by partially freezing Doppledock and then removing the ice. This concentrates the flavors, resulting in a dark brown beer with an average ABV of 9–13%. The flavors are rich, sweet with hints of chocolate and balanced with the high alcohol presence.

Helles Lagers are often referred to as the Munich Original Lager, and are golden blond with nice effervescence and range in ABV from 4.7–5.4%. The flavor is malty and dry with lingering hop notes.

Oktoberfest Märzen is typically amber in color with malty, clean flavors with a dry finish. Marzen is an amber lager that is the classic beer of autumn. Mellow and very drinkable, with a malty taste and a dry finish. Pairs perfectly with fall foods, including roasted meats, sausages, and even chili.

Schwarzbier is a less popular variety, but nonetheless is a noteworthy beer. These are medium-bodied dark lagers. Schwarzbiers have a clean lager taste with hints of chocolate, coffee, and vanilla. They are well-balanced and have a subtle hop bitterness. The Vienna Lager is a reddish-brown lager with a strong malty flavor.

Of course, today the most popular lager is the Pilsner. Like many beer varieties, the first pilsner was created with a stroke of luck. In 1842, the Bavarian brewer Josef Groll traveled to Plzen in Bohemia, where he brewed a lighter beer that turned out golden, light, and easy to drink, due to the unique combination of the regions soft water and local barley. Today, pilsners are produced all around the world. Pilsners are a great meal starter, setting the stage with a light touch before marching on to deeper, more complex flavors.

PORTER

Porter is a strong, dark beer generally made with brown malt and spiced pretty evenly with hops. Smoked malts, coffee, or chocolate are also often used to complement the toasted, some would even say burnt, flavor. This is a very accommodating beer, and it is common to find it mixed with flavors like pumpkin, nuts, or even bourbon. Porters are great in sauces, meats, and even pair nicely with chocolate desserts.

STOUT

In old England, the word stout meant "proud" or "brave," and became associated with "strong." Brewers in England and Ireland began labeling their porters as "stout" to advertise their stronger ABVs and flavors. These beers are toasted and dark, with chocolate and coffee undertones. They have a beautiful head and are a favorite in our kitchen for stews and strongly flavored dishes or desserts.

HYBRID BEERS

Many hybrid beers could fall into the lager category, but there is a wide variation in the ways they are processed. Many of them speak to the technique used, such as Anchor Brewing's "steam beers" or smoked and wood-aged techniques.

Other beers rely on fruits, vegetables, or herbs and spices to achieve their unique results. In some cases, these flavorings replace hops, in others, they are added to the hops.

Lambic derives its unique flavor from spontaneous fermentation by wild yeasts. Delicious, dry, and fruity with a slightly sour undertone. Fresh, whole fruit is often a component. Lambic is best served cold.

Then there are the Champagne-style beers. These beers use the traditional method of making Champagne and sparkling wines, with the second fermentation taking place right in the bottle. These beers share the small soft bubbles of sparkling wine, but retain the flavor and color of beer. A really special way to celebrate!

COOKING WITH BEER

Cooking with beer should be a fun and creative process, but there are a couple of guidelines that will help make experimentation a success.

ONE FOR YOU, ONE FOR THE POT
Never cook with a beer you wouldn't want to drink. The very characteristic that you don't enjoy is likely the one that will emerge in your recipe.

MATCHING FLAVORS AND WEIGHT
The flavor profile of a beer is essential when making a great pairing. Find beer with similar flavors as the food you intend to cook, or that have flavors that will complement one another. The best way to create a perfect pairing is to incorporate a little of the beer into the dish you are preparing. This creates a "bridge" in flavor and will enhance both the food and beer flavors while enjoying them together.

When pairing your meal with a great beer, it is important to consider the weight of the beer and the weight of the food. Pair light with light and heavy with heavy. Stews pair well with heavy dark, malty beers while salads prefer light wheat beers or lagers.

We have paired all of our recipes with particular beers throughout the book. While we love these choices, we also know that not every market will offer all of our picks. So if we pair a dish with an IPA, simply replace our choice with the most similar IPA in your area. As long your substitution is in the same category, your results should be good. And if you happen to have a favorite in the category, your results may even be better!

TENDERIZING AND DRESSINGS

The alcohol in beer has enough acid to break down the proteins in meat, but not as much as the vinegar or citrus juices that are often used. This makes it a great base for your steak marinade, tenderizing while maintaining the texture of the meat. If you are looking for tenderizing without a lot of flavor notes, use a lighter beer. If you want the beer to influence the flavor, go for darker beers that will add some caramelized tones behind. For fish, chicken, or seafood, try a nice hefeweizen. Marinate for at least an hour before grilling. Salad dressings are also a perfect way to incorporate a beer into a light dish. Depending on the salad we find that Imperial IPAs, Wheat beers and Pilsner all work to replace the acidity in a traditional vinaigrette.

BAKING

Baking is one of the places where you can really have fun with your desserts! Beers such as Imperial IPAs, lambics, Dobbledocks, Eisbocks, stouts, and Porters have become some of our favorite beers to incorporate into desserts. When combining beer and dessert, pair similar flavor profiles together. If the beer is citrusy, like an Imperial IPA, incorporate it into a lemony or fruit-based dessert. The sugar in the dessert will balance out the hoppy bitterness and you will be left with a perfect pairing and a complex, delicious dessert. Beers with strong coffee notes work perfectly with coffee- and chocolate-flavored desserts. Maple, caramel, and raspberry all stand up well too. When I use a strongly carbonated beer in baked goods, I prefer to boil the carbonation and alcohol off,

cool it completely, and then add it to the desired recipe. This allows the beer flavor to come through without accidently activating your leavening agents before you intend to.

DE-GLAZING

The sugars in beer make it a great de-glazing agent. Use a darker beer with less hops to add richness and a note of sweetness to the pan. Be careful about using a hoppy beer; it will leave behind bitter flavors.

FRYING

Why is beer-battered fish so awesome? The secret is the beer, of course! The yeast in the beer works as a leavening agent, creating a batter that is light and crisps beautifully when fried. And of course, the beer adds that extra bit of flavor that bridges nicely with the beer you are drinking.

GRILLING

Smoky grilled meat + beer = awesome! Marinate your meat in beer, pre-steam your sausages, mop with beer barbecue sauce, even throw a splash of beer on your meat as it cooks. What could be more natural? Not only that, but adding beer to your grilling process actually inhibits some of the carcinogenic effects of charring meat.

SIMMERING

Simmering a dish will consolidate the flavor of the beer and influence the taste. The malt and the hops of the beer will show themselves clearly. Malty beers will enhance the richness of soups and stews, and kick up the flavor of many desserts. Hops, on the other hand, can make a nice stew bitter. Hoppy beers are better used in light dishes, sauces, brines, or marinades. If you use a hoppy beer in a stew, finish it quickly at the end of cooking.

STEAMING AND POACHING

Our hot dogs and sausages are always steamed in a nice wheat beer, adding a delicate flavor or imparting a wonderful aroma to the meats. Poaching is also a beautiful way to cook a delicate piece of fish with your favorite light beer.

This book is broken up into four seasons: winter, spring, summer, and autumn. We have put together five menus for each season. Each menu highlights the seasonal, fresh ingredients of a particular season. We hope this book will be considered a resource for all your dinner and party needs. Take a whole chapter as inspiration and execute it in its entirety or simply pick and choose the recipes you need for any given night. These menus do not have to be prepared all at once. Interested in a light dinner, the poached sole will do the trick. We have included a number of salad recipes and vinaigrettes, soup, vegetable side dishes, meats, seafood, cookies, and more complex desserts. We hope you enjoy cooking your way through this book as much as we have enjoyed putting it together!

WINTER

What better way to celebrate winter than with rich food and hearty beer? The menus in this section celebrate the best in cold weather cooking, from comfort food like rich beef stews and roasted meats to root vegetables and fresh seafood.

SALUTE TO BELGIUM—THE BEGINNING OF BEER

Belgium is a small country with a long history, and with food and beer at its very heart. Some of the best beers still made in Belgium trace their history back 300 years. It could be argued that the tradition of craft beer originated here. Six Trappist monasteries continue the tradition today, five of which are located in Belgium.

Although beer may have had its origins in the Belgium church, Trappist beers are not the only types of great beer you can find in Belgium. Belgian beer consists of as many as eighteen varieties, and are considered among the very best in the world. Varieties include Abbey Ale, Amber Ale, Belgium Strong Ale, Brown Ale, Dubbel, Faro beer, Golden Ale, Gueuze, Kriek beer, Lambic, Oud Bruin, Pilsner, Red beer, Saison Ale, Stout, Tripel and White Ale. Of course, these varieties are not unique to Belgium alone, but many of the beers being produced today have found inspiration in the original brewing traditions of Belgium.

A handful of our favorites are showcased in this chapter, but you are not limited to our pairing choices! We encourage you to take these examples and run with them. Stay true to the flavor profile we have provided, to get a true pairing experience. For example, if you can't find Wittekerke in your area, then pair the mussels with another witbier of your choice.

In this chapter we highlight classic Belgian dishes. If you have visited this region, you will recognize some of these classics. We have put our own twist on all of these dishes, but have kept the essence of the original dish.

SALUTE TO BELGIUM MENU
1st Course
   Prince Edward Island Mussels steamed in saison, red coconut curry cream with french fries
   Wittekerke, BrouwerijBavik, Belgium
2nd Course
   Flemish Carbonnade- Slow braised in brown ale with smashed red bliss potatoes and roasted shallots.
   Leffe Brown, Abbaye de Leffe, Belgium
3rd Course
   Chocolate raspberry swirl brownie, raspberry Lambic ice cream with cherries, chocolate ganache, fresh raspberries, and Cherish whipped cream
   Cherish Raspberry Belgium Lambic, Brouwerij Van Steenberge, Belgium

FEATURED BEERS

WITTEKERKE

Made by: BrouwerijBavik
Style: Witbier
From: Belgium
5% ABV
Served in a shaker

    This naturally cloudy, unfiltered beer has a golden straw color with a thick off-white head. Very light and refreshing, it pairs perfectly with seafood, salad, or spicy food. Best served cold.

LEFFE BROWN

Made by: Abbaye de Leffe S.A.
Style: Belgian Dark Ale
From: Belgium
6.5% ABV
Serve in a beer chalice

    This is the original Leffe beer. It was first made in 1240 as a way of purifying contaminated drinking water. This beer pours dark brown with a creamy head. The complex caramelized, vanilla, coffee, roasted flavors have a lightly bitter finish. This beer pairs perfectly with caramelized flavors, braised meats, creamy dishes, and even desserts with chocolate or coffee.

CHERISH RASPBERRY LAMBIC

Made by: Brouwerij Van Steenberge
Style: Fruit Lambic
From: Belgium
5% ABV
Serve in a beer chalice or champagne glass

    This fruit beer holds a perfect balance between sweet and sour, finishing with a light raspberry. It pours a delightful red-amber color, and is great on its own or paired with salads, fruit desserts, ice cream, and chocolate.

RECIPES

COCONUT CREAM AND RED CURRY BEER MUSSELS

These mussels are so good. They are sweet and just a little spicy. The sauce is divine and you will find yourself soaking your last morsels of bread and French fries into the remaining sauce long after the mussels have disappeared. We prefer Prince Edward Island mussels because of their size and quality. They pair beautifully with a light Belgium Saison or HefeWeizen.

Serves 2 people
1 pound mussels, picked and cleaned
12 ounces coconut cream
$1/2$ stalk lemon grass, crushed
2 teaspoons red curry paste or powder
1 tablespoon unsalted butter
$1/4$ tablespoon garlic, minced
$1/4$ tablespoon shallots, minced
2 ounces beer
2 leaves basil, chiffonade

Reduce the coconut cream by one third over low heat. Add the crushed lemongrass and stir in the red curry paste. This sauce can be made ahead of time and stored for 3 days.

Clean the mussels. This process should start with a freshness check. Pick through mussels to make sure they are all alive. Fresh live mussels should be tightly closed or readily close up when lightly tapped on a table. Discard any open mussels that do not close. Soak mussels for 20 minutes in cold water to filter and clean themselves. Remove the beard (those little brown threads near the hinge of mussel) by pulling gently out and down towards the hinge of the shell. Wash the outside of the shells thoroughly in cold running water until all debris is gone. Pat dry.

Add butter to hot sauté pan, add shallots and garlic, and cook for 1 minute or until translucent. Add mussels, coconut cream, and beer, mix well, and cover. Cook until all shells have opened about 3–5 minutes.

Remove from pan and serve in a mussel pot with basil on top. Serve with a side of thick cut French fries.

(Crushing lemongrass is easy. Start first by cutting off the end bulb and removing the tough outer leaves, cut into thirds and pound the stalk with the side of your knife, scrape all the stalk into the cream, and steep for 1 hour covered with plastic wrap. When steeping is complete, strain out the lemongrass)

FRENCH FRIES

Double-cooked French fries in the classic tradition are certainly a labor of love. Vigilance is key to the success of house-made fries, but the effort is worth every bite.

Serves 4 people

2 pounds Idaho potatoes or other baking potato, cut $1/4$" x $1/4$". We change potato varieties seasonally, but are partial to the flavor and texture of Yukon Gold potatoes. $1/2$ gallon high quality fryer oil, such as peanut oil, vegetable oil, soy oil, duck fat, or lard

Begin by peeling and cutting the potatoes in even $1/4$"x $1/4$" pieces. Soak them in cold water for 15 minutes and then drain thoroughly. This step removes a lot of the starch, which is crucial to producing a firm, crispy batch of fries.

Preheat your fryer and fill with oil. Countertop fryers are a convenient investment, especially if you make fries often, but a large stock pot with a high temp thermometer is also suitable.

Bring the oil to 275 degrees. Blanch potatoes in your heated fryer oil for about four minutes. This step is meant to cook the potatoes, not to crisp them. Use a slotted utensil to remove them from the oil, and immediately place them on kitchen paper or a sheet tray fitted with a wire rack. Drain excess grease and allow to rest for at least 20 minutes.

(At this point, you may wrap the blanched potatoes with plastic wrap, poking holes in the wrap to provide some ventilation. Chill in the refrigerator until ready to use, up to 24 hours.)

When you are ready to serve your fries, heat your oil to 350 degrees and fry the blanched potatoes a second time. This step takes only 2–3 minutes, or until potatoes are golden brown and crispy.

Remove promptly and place on kitchen paper to absorb excess oil. Season with fine ground sea salt and black pepper. Serve immediately.

(If you are cooking for a crowd, work in small batches to ensure even browning. Browning time depends on the heat of your oil, as well as the sugar and moisture content of your potatoes, so cooking time may vary.)

RED BLISS SMASHED POTATOES

These potatoes are rich and creamy. Smashing them instead of whipping creates a hardy texture and preserves some chunky potato pieces.

Serves 6-8
1¹/₂ pounds red bliss potatoes
¹/₄ cup unsalted butter
¹/₃ cup heavy cream
1 teaspoon salt
1 teaspoon pepper, fresh ground

Fill a large stockpot with the potatoes and cool water. Simmer potatoes in salted water. Cover and cook until potatoes are fork tender, about 30 minutes. Drain the potatoes in a large colander and return to the stockpot.

Melt the butter and cream together in a medium saucepan over low heat. Fold the cream mix gently into the hot potatoes. Add salt and pepper and lightly smash with a potato masher. Serve immediately.

FLEMISH CARBONNADE

This is true comfort food! It is rich, hearty, and completely satisfying. This dish is great for cold nights. Pair with creamy smashed potatoes and roasted shallots. This pairs very well with a brown Belgium ale.

Serves 4-6 people

10 ounces peppered hickory smoked bacon, cut into 1/2 inch pieces

2 tablespoons all-purpose flour

1 1/2 pounds beef chuck roast, cut into 2-inch cubes

1 tablespoon sea salt

1 teaspoon black pepper, ground

2 tablespoons extra virgin olive oil

1 medium yellow onion, medium dice

1 large carrot, medium dice

2 stalks celery, medium dice

4 cloves garlic, minced

1 tablespoon whole grain mustard

12 ounces dark beer

2 cups beef stock

10 prunes, whole

1 green apple, medium dice

Heat a Dutch oven or thick bottomed large skillet (we prefer cast iron) over medium heat and add the bacon. Render the fat slowly until fat melts into the pan and meat is crispy, about 8 minutes. Remove the bacon and drain. Reserve.

Coat the beef with the flour, salt, and pepper. Brown the beef in the bacon fat on all sides until golden brown. Remove from pot. Reserve.

Using the same pot, reduce the heat to medium, and add the olive oil. Add the onion, carrot, celery, and garlic. De-glaze the pot with a splash of beer. Sauté the vegetables until they begin to soften.

Return the bacon and beef to the pot. Add the beer, beef, stock, and mustard. Bring the pot to a boil. Partially cover the pot and simmer on medium heat.

After 45 minutes of cooking time, add the prunes. Continue cooking for 20 minutes and then skim the top removing extra grease. Cook for another 15 minutes, then add the apple. Continue cooking stew for another 15 minutes or until the beef is fork tender. Serve with smashed potatoes and roasted shallots.

CHOCOLATE RASPBERRY SWIRL BROWNIE

Incredibly rich and delicious. They can be made with or without the raspberry swirl. I love to pair these with a black cherry Lambic ice cream and ganache.

Makes a 8" x 8" pan
1 cup fresh raspberries
¹/₄ cup sugar
2 tablespoons raspberry or cherry Lambic

¹/₄ pound unsalted butter, melted
2 tablespoons raspberry or cherry Lambic
³/₄ cup sugar
¹/₂ cup dark brown sugar
2 large eggs
¹/₄ teaspoon sea salt
¹/₂ cup cocoa powder
³/₄ cup all-purpose flour
¹/₂ cup dark chocolate chips

Begin by making the raspberry puree. Combine raspberries, sugar and Lambic in a medium saucepan. Cook over medium-high heat, stirring occasionally, until raspberries break down and begin to boil with the sugar and Lambic. Reduce this mixture by ¹/₂ and remove from heat. Let cool about 15 minutes and puree in blender until smooth. Set aside.

Preheat oven to 350 degrees. Combine salt, cocoa powder, and flour in a bowl and set aside. Bring 2 tablespoons of Lambic to a boil in small saucepan. Turn off heat, and add the butter and allow to melt.

In a mixer bowl combine the Lambic-butter mix with the white and brown sugars. Add eggs one at a time, incorporating them thoroughly into the mix. Add the cocoa/flour mixture in 2 separate batches, combining the first half thoroughly before adding the second batch. Stir in the chocolate chips.

Pour the batter into a greased 8x8 baking dish, using the back of a spoon to level it. Dollop the cooled raspberry puree on top of the brownies mix, and swirl it into the batter with a butter knife. Do not over-mix; the swirls of raspberry should remain visible.

Bake for about 30 minutes. Set aside and cool. Serve with black cherry Lambic ice cream, ganache and a garnish of whipped cream.

DARK CHOCOLATE GANACHE

A versatile chocolate sauce that can be used anytime you want to add a note of chocolate to a dessert. It's wonderful over ice cream and desserts, or you can whip it to create a light cake filling. This recipe includes a cherry-raspberry Lambic, but feel free to switch this ingredient with another beer or liquor to help bridge the flavor of your dish.

Makes 2 cups
1 cup dark chocolate (I prefer 60–70 percent cocoa flavor)
1 cup heavy cream
2 tablespoons beer

Put the chocolate in a separate medium bowl. Bring cream and beer to a simmer in a medium saucepan. When cream reaches a simmer, pour over the chocolate, and whisk until all the chocolate is melted and the mix looks smooth and shinny. Serve this sauce warm. Store in an airtight container for 3–5 days.

FRESH WHIPPED CREAM

Fresh whipped cream is so easy to make and worth the little bit of extra effort. This recipe can be flavored with anything from lemon zest, cocoa powder, beer, liquor, vanilla . . . the list goes on and on. We are pairing this with our cherry Lambic ice cream and chocolate brownie.

Makes 2 cups
1 cup heavy whipping cream, cold
1/4 cup powdered sugar
1 tablespoon beer (or vanilla, other flavorings)

Combine the cream, sugar, and flavoring in a cold, large mixing bowl. Be sure your cream and mixing bowl are cold. If either is warm, you will have a hard time creating the desired texture. Whisk until the cream creates soft peaks and looks light and fluffy. This only takes a couple of minutes in an electric mixer, but can be done by hand with a little extra effort. Be careful not to overbeat. Serve immediately.

CHERRY LAMBIC ICE CREAM

Homemade ice cream may seem like an unnecessary luxury with all the gourmet ice creams on the market. But there is nothing that compares with custards and ice cream infused with your favorite beer. It creates a unique depth of flavor that you can't get anywhere else. The Lambic cream and cherries pair really well with the gooey chocolate raspberry swirl brownies and topped with ganache.

Makes 4 cups

1 1/2 cups halved pitted sweet cherries
2 tablespoons sugar
4 tablespoons Lambic

1 1/2 cups heavy cream
1 cup whole milk
1/2 cup sugar
1/4 teaspoon sea salt
3 tablespoons Lambic
6 large egg yolks

Start by cooking the cherries. Cook halved pitted cherries, 2 tablespoons sugar, and 4 tablespoons Lambic in a small saucepan over medium heat, stirring occasionally, until syrupy, 8–10 minutes. Cool and set aside.

Next make the ice cream base. Combine 1 1/2 cups heavy cream, 1 cup whole milk, 3 tablespoons Lambic, 1/4 cup sugar, and a pinch of salt in a medium saucepan. Bring mixture just to a simmer and remove from heat.

In a separate medium bowl, whisk the egg yolks and the remaining 1/4 cup sugar until all combined. Gradually temper the warm cream mixture into the egg mix by adding the warm cream one ladle at a time, whisking constantly until all cream is combined with eggs. Return to the pot and cook over medium heat, stirring constantly, until it becomes thick enough to coat the back of a wooden spoon, about 3 minutes. Strain ice cream base through a fine chinois into a medium bowl set over a bowl of ice. Allow to cool, stirring occasionally.

When ice cream base is cool, stir in the cherry mix. Process the base in an ice cream maker according to manufacturer's instructions. Store in airtight container in your freezer.

WINTER SOLSTICE DINNER

We embrace the weather, the short days and the chill in the air, and welcome into our home the elements that most nourish us this time of year. These include a warm fire burning in the fireplace, roasted squash, chestnuts over the fire, and plenty of stuffing and dark chocolate walnuts.

Our menus are based on local, seasonal ingredients. This menu is taken straight from the root cellar, and celebrates the hearty vegetables that winter offers us.

Of course, the beers we have chosen are specially designed for cold weather drinking, and will warm the soul and satisfy any pallet. Enjoy!

WINTER SOLSTICE MENU

1st Course
Roasted Butternut Squash Tart with honey, goat cheese, and toasted seeds
Hobgoblin ESB-Wychwood Brewery Company, UK

2nd Course
Confit of Chicken with chestnut and smoked bacon stuffing, brussels sprouts, thyme-curieux jus
Allagash Curieux, Bourbon Barrel-Aged Tripel, Allagash Brewery, Maine

3rd Course
Indulgent Chocolate Praline Layer Cake with layered walnut praline, chocolate cream, ganache, candied walnuts
Chocolate Stout, Rogue Ales, Oregon

FEATURED BEERS

HOBGOBLIN

Made by: Wychwood Brewery Company
Style: ESB- Strong Bitter
From: England
5.20% ABV
Serve in an English pint

   This beer pours copper red and is well balanced with strong roasted malt, hoppy bitterness, mild fruity, and toffee flavors. This beer pairs well with roasted and grilled vegetables, stews, and burgers.

CURIEUX—BOURBON BARREL AGED TRIPEL

Made by: Allagash Brewing
Style: Tripel Bourbon Barrel Aged Strong Ale
From: Maine
11% ABV
Serve in a beer a Trappist glass or tulip

   This pours light golden color with a white head. It is quite light, considering that it was aged for 8 weeks in Jim Beam Bourbon barrels. It has a flavor profile with lots of oaky character, caramel, coconut, vanilla, and of course, light bourbon. This beer is smooth, but definitely packs a punch. Pairs well with pork, chicken, and duck.

CHOCOLATE INDULGENCE

Chocolate Stout
Made by: Rogue Ales
Style: Stout
From: Oregon
6% ABV
Serve in an English pint

   This beer tastes of pure Belgium dark chocolate, the thick tan head and dark brown color enhance that chocolate flavor and bitter cocoa finish, this beer smells roasted, spicy and has a hint of coffee. No one can argue that this beer pairs beautifully with dessert.

RECIPES

ROASTED BUTTERNUT SQUASH TART

This tart is well-balanced, with a light flaky puff pastry base anchoring the creamy texture of perfectly roasted squash. Add a hint of honey, beer, and goat cheese and it becomes a real crowd pleaser. Make these bite-sized for a cocktail party or larger and serve as a first course.

Serves 6 people
10 ounces puff pastry, use frozen or fresh
1 small butternut squash, about 1 pound
2 tablespoons olive oil
1 teaspoon cumin
1 teaspoon cayenne pepper
1 teaspoon sea salt
$1/2$ teaspoon pepper
$1/2$ cup goat cheese, crumbled
$1/4$ cup honey
1 teaspoons beer

Preheat oven to 375 degrees. If using frozen puff pastry thaw for about 20 minutes.

Prepare butternut squash for baking. Peel the squash with a paring knife or strong peeler. Cut the squash in half and remove the seeds, reserve seeds for toasting. Cut the squash into $1/2$ inch pieces and combine in medium bowl with the cumin, cayenne pepper, salt, pepper, and oil. Mix to coat all the pieces and spread squash out in single layer on baking sheet. Bake at 375 degrees for 15–20 minutes or until fork tender. Remove and allow to cool.

When squash is still a little warm, evenly distribute across the puff pastry sheet. Spread the goat cheese crumbles across the tart in areas the squash is not. Bake in oven for about 25 minutes or until pastry begins to raise and turn golden brown and crispy. Remove from oven.

Combine the honey and beer. When tart is ready to serve drizzle the honey-beer mix over the tart, sprinkle with toasted and seasoned squash seeds and cut. Serve immediately.

ORANGE-CURIEUX CONFIT CHICKEN AND THYME-CURIEUX JUS

Planning ahead is essential with this dish. The chicken needs to develop flavor in the fat for a minimum of 24 hours and up to 2 weeks. The longer the better, this cooking technique is a preservation method, but it is also a very effective method of infusing flavor and creating a juicy, tender piece of meat.

Serves 4 people

4 chicken leg quarters (thighs and legs still attached)
Sea salt and pepper
6 cups fat (chicken fat, duck fat or lard)
1 cup strong ale
2 white onions, thinly sliced
2 oranges, thinly sliced
4 bay leaves
4 garlic cloves
10 whole peppercorns
2 sprigs fresh thyme
6 cups fat (chicken fat, duck fat, or lard)

Get a large, heavy bottom skillet very hot. Season the chicken on all sides with sea salt and freshly ground pepper. Melt a tablespoon of fat in the skillet and sear the chicken to a medium brown color on all sides. Remove skillet from heat and set the chicken aside.

In a large Dutch oven, layer the onion slices, orange slices, bay leaves, garlic, and peppercorns. Lay the chicken in a single layer on the onion-orange layer. Warm the 6 cups of fat until liquefied. Pour it over the chicken, being sure to cover the chicken completely. Simmer on medium heat for 2 hours, completely submerged in the oil. Add 1 cup of beer and continue simmering for 10 minutes. Remove from the heat and cool. Refrigerate for a minimum of 24 hours and up to 2 weeks.

To make the jus, carefully remove the block of fat that has separated from the gelatinous stock in the bottom of the pan. This fat should come out easily and what remains is the chicken stock and spices. Remove the stock at the bottom of the pan and put in a clean saucepan. Gently heat the stock and strain out the oranges and other flavorings. Add fresh thyme and set aside. Right before serving this chicken dish, warm the jus and finish with a splash of beer.

When ready to serve the chicken, remove it carefully from the fat, keeping the fat cold. Set the chicken pieces aside. Preheat the new, clean 6 cups of fat in the clean Dutch oven to 340 degrees. Carefully add the chicken to the hot oil and fry for about 6 minutes or until golden brown and crunchy. Serve hot with jus.

CHESTNUT AND SMOKED BACON STUFFING

This stuffing is smoky and nutty, our twist on a classic dish.

Serves 4 people

$1/2$ pound chestnuts, roasted and peeled

$1/2$ pound smoked bacon, cut into $1/4$ inch pieces

$1/4$ pound unsalted butter

$1/2$ cup white onion, small dice

1 clove garlic, minced

$1/4$ cup carrots, peeled and small dice

$1/4$ cup celery, small dice

4 sprigs fresh thyme

4 sprigs fresh tarragon

4 sprigs fresh parsley leaves

$1/8$ teaspoon nutmeg

1 teaspoon sea salt

1 teaspoon pepper

1 pound white bread, dried out, crust removed and cut into $1/2$ inch cubes

1 cup chicken stock

Preheat the oven to 425 degrees. Clean the chestnuts. Using a sharp knife, cut an x in the top of the raw nuts to help the steam release as they begin to roast. Arrange the nuts on a baking sheet and roast for 20–25 minutes. They should be tender and easy to peel. Cool nuts and peel the shell off, set aside.

Place cut bacon into a large, cold sauté pan. Heat covered over medium-low heat, rendering the bacon until the fat is melted and translucent. Remove the cover and increase the heat to medium high and finish cooking the bacon until it becomes brown and crunchy. Add the butter and melt. Add the onions, garlic, carrots, celery, fresh herbs, nutmeg, salt, and pepper. Stir to combine all the ingredients. Cook for about 5 minutes or until the carrots are fork tender. Add the bread cubes and stir until combined. Mix in the chicken stock.

Transfer the stuffing to a baking dish and bake in the oven at 350 degrees for about 15–20 minutes or until top get a nice golden brown crunch.

BROWN BUTTER BRUSSELS SPROUTS

Brussels sprouts are one of the most misunderstood vegetables, but because they keep so well, they are one of the green stars of our winter menus. And when cooked properly, they can really wow even the biggest critics. Try this recipe and you will see.

Serves 4 people

1 1/2 pounds Brussels sprouts, cleaned and quartered
1 gallon water
3 tablespoons kosher salt
2 tablespoons unsalted butter
1/2 teaspoon sea salt
1/2 teaspoon black pepper

Clean the Brussels sprouts by peeling any discolored or damaged outer leaves. In a medium bowl, soak the sprouts in warm water for about 10 minutes. This helps release any dirt in the inner leaves. Strain the sprouts and rinse with cold water. Cut the tough stem off the bottom of the sprout. Be sure not to cut the leaves to prevent the sprouts from falling apart. Cut the sprouts in quarters if large, or in halves if smaller in size.

Bring 1 gallon of water to a boil with 3 tablespoons of salt. Pour the Brussels sprouts into boiling water and cook uncovered for about 8 minutes. The sprouts should be fork tender, but not mushy; they should have some resistance when poked with a fork.

While Brussels sprouts are cooking, prepare an ice bath in a large bowl with cold water and plenty of ice. Remove spouts from the boiling water, strain, and immediately pour into the ice bath to stop the cooking.

When ready to serve, strain and pat dry the Brussels sprouts. In a medium sauté pan, lightly brown the butter. Sauté the sprouts in the brown butter lightly for about 1 1/2 minutes or until they are warm. Finish with salt and pepper. Serve immediately.

INDULGENT CHOCOLATE PRALINE LAYER CAKE

Indulgent, decadent, rich and creamy—and perfect with beer. This cake is complex and unique, and remarkably delicious paired with a chocolate-flavored beer.

Makes 16 pieces

Layer 1

2 cups chocolate cookie crumbs, see page 28

$1/2$ cup unsalted butter

Layer 2

$1^1/_2$ cups unsalted butter

1 cup dark brown sugar

1 tablespoon beer

1 cup chopped walnuts, toasted and chopped

Layer 3

16 ounces cream cheese

$1/_2$ cup powdered sugar

$1/_2$ cup dark brown sugar

3 tablespoons cocoa powder

2 tablespoons beer

Layer 4

1 cup dark chocolate chips, 60%

$1/_2$ cup heavy cream

1 tablespoon beer

Layer 1: Preheat oven to 350 degrees. Melt 1/2 cup of butter and combine in a small bowl with chocolate cookie crumbs. Evenly press into the bottom of a greased 9 inch spring form pan. Bake at 350 degrees for 10 minutes. Let cool while preparing other layers.

Layer 2: In a large saucepan over medium heat, melt $1^1/_2$ cups of butter and add the brown sugar. Bring this mix to a boil, stirring constantly. Reduce heat to low and simmer for 10 minutes. Remove from the heat and stir in beer. Stir toasted walnuts into praline mix and immediately pour onto cookie crust in the spring form pan. Spread out evenly and refrigerate for 1–2 hours or until set.

Layer 3: In medium bowl combine sugars and the cocoa powder. Then in a large mixing bowl

with the paddle attachment beat together the cream cheese, sugar mix, and beer until smooth. Spread this mix evenly over the praline layer and refrigerate for 1–2 hours or until set.

Layer 4: In a small saucepan, simmer cream and beer. Put chocolate in a small bowl and pour the cream mix over chocolate; whisk until smooth. Let cool for about 10 minutes and pour over the cream cheese filling. Refrigerate for 1–2 hours or until set.

Carefully run a knife around edge of pan to loosen; remove the spring form pan and slice using a hot knife. Garnish with candied walnuts. Keep this cake refrigerated.

CANDIED WALNUTS

This recipe makes a great garnish for salads and desserts, but our friends love to munch them right out of the bowl.

Makes ¹/₂ cup
¹/₂ cup walnuts, lightly toasted
¹/₈ cup sugar
1 teaspoon water

Mix the sugar and water into a small saucepan. Cook sugar on medium heat (do not stir the sugar), and cook until the color is a medium amber brown. As soon as sugar is a medium amber brown color, add the walnuts to the pan, quickly stirring and coating each piece with the sugar mixture.

Spread the walnuts out on a greased baking sheet. Separate the walnuts from each other using a fork or other utensil. This needs to be done quickly to prevent sugar from hardening the nuts together. Let cool completely.

DARK CHOCOLATE COOKIES

Great cookies for munching, a simpler variation without the chocolate chips is perfect for cookie crumbs for cakes and pies.

Makes 12 cookies
¹/₂ cup unsalted butter, softened
³/₄ cup dark brown sugar, packed
1 large egg
1 tablespoon of beer
1 teaspoon vanilla
1 cup all-purpose flour
¹/₃ cup cocoa powder
1 teaspoon baking soda
¹/₂ teaspoon sea salt
2 cups dark chocolate chips, optional

Preheat oven to 325 degrees.

Cream the butter and brown sugar together in a large mixing bowl with the paddle attachment. When butter mix is soft and fluffy, add the egg, beer, and vanilla, mixing until incorporated. In separate bowl combine the flour, baking soda, cocoa powder, and salt. Add the dry ingredients in two stages, mixing until just incorporated. Stir in the chocolate chips.

Drop large dollops of the dough about 3 inches apart onto a greased baking sheet. Bake for 16–18 minutes. The tops will begin to look cracked. Cool on baking sheets.

Variation: For baking the cookies to use as crumbs, skip the chocolate chips. Bake dollops of dough for about 20 minutes. Cool cookies completely and process to fine crumbs in a food processor.

HOLIDAY PARTY

This time of year, we never miss an opportunity to get people together for dinner, whether it is a warm and cozy Sunday night supper or an extravagant multi-course meal. This menu is warm, comforting, and completely satisfying. It also has a surprising ending—a dessert that is so good and pairs so well with beer that it actually makes our guests laugh with delight.

HOLIDAY PARTY MENU
1st Course:

    Maple and Blue Cheese Sliced Filet Bruschetta

    The Maple Collaboration, Peak Organic Brewing Company, Maine

2nd Course:

    Chorizo Stuffed Pork Loin with sweet potato gratin, broccoli rabe, scotch ale sauce

    Skull Splitter Scotch Ale, Orkney Brewery, United Kingdom

3rd Course:

    Baked Alaska, with creamy lemon sorbet, red currant coulis, burnt meringue

    1809 Berliner Weisse, Professor Fritz Briem, Germany

FEATURED BEERS

THE MAPLE COLLABORATION
Made by: Peak Organic
Style: Red Ale
From: Maine
6.7% ABV
Serve in a beer an english pint

This complex maple beer pours copper in color. With a medium bodied mouthfeel, this beer comes across with complex maltiness balanced out with hop bitterness and sweet maple syrup. Pair this with maple syrup, roasted meats, and cheese.

SKULL SPLITTER SCOTCH ALE
Made by: Orkney Brewery
Style: Wee Heavy Barrel Aged Strong Ale
From: United Kingdom
8.5% ABV
Serve in thistle glass

This beer pours a tawny-red color. The taste is of sweet toasted malt, molasses, dried fruit, and spices. This beer pairs well with pork, strong cheeses, cream, and pate.

1809 BERLINER WEISSE
Made by: Professor Fritz Briem
Style: Berliner Weisse
From: Germany
5% ABV
Serve in a bowl or bolleke glass

This sour beer pours a pale golden color. It tastes of light lactic acid, citrus, unmalted wheat, and cloves. This beer pairs with light citrus desserts, cream, and berries.

RECIPES

MAPLE AND BLUE CHEESE SLICED BEEF FILET BRUSCHETTA

Sweet maple and tangy blue cheese combine to make a delightful bite. Serve this appetizer passed before dinner, or plated as a first course.

Makes 1 dozen bruschetta

1 pound beef tenderloin, trimmed
1 baguette
4 tablespoons olive oil
Sea salt and pepper
3 ounces blue cheese
3 tablespoons real maple syrup
2 teaspoons maple beer

Preheat oven to 400 degrees. Salt and pepper the trimmed beef filet. In a hot pan, add 2 tablespoons olive oil. Sear the beef on one side for 2 minutes and then turn over and sear for another 2 minutes. Finish the filet in the oven until it reaches medium-rare or about 130 degrees. Remove it and let rest.

Slice the baguette in $1/4$ inch slices. Place it in a medium bowl and mix the baguette slices with 2 tablespoons oil, salt, and pepper to taste. Layer a baking sheet with the bread in a single layer and toast in the oven for 2 minutes. Remove, flip the pieces and return to the oven to toast the other side of the bread about two more minutes. Be careful not to overcook the bread; it is best if it is still soft but toasted. Set aside to cool.

Mix the maple syrup and beer together in a small bowl.

To assemble the bruschetta, slice the beef in $1/4$ inch slices and place the beef slices on the toasted bread. Crumble the blue cheese onto the bruschetta, distributing it evenly among all 12 of the bruschetta, about $1/4$ ounce each. Place under the broiler at medium heat to partially melt the cheese. Remove before the cheese is completely melted. Drizzle the maple-beer mix over the bruschetta and serve immediately.

CHORIZO STUFFED PORK LOIN WITH SCOTCH ALE SAUCE

The chorizo in this dish adds a smoky complexity to a simple roasted pork loin. We have paired this with a creamy sweet potato gratin to balance out the spicy and salty elements of the chorizo.

Serves 8 people

3–4 pounds pork loin, trimmed
1 pound chorizo
1 teaspoon olive oil
Salt and pepper to taste
$1/2$ cup unsalted butter
$1/2$ cup scotch ale
Salt and pepper to taste

Preheat oven to 450 degrees. Butterfly the pork loin and stuff with the chorizo, salt, and pepper. Tie the loin together with kitchen string. In a roasting pan coat the bottom with olive oil and cook for 15 minutes. Drop oven temperature to 375 degrees and cook until internal temperature of the roast reaches 150 degrees. Remove from the oven and let rest. Slice the pork loin and serve with sweet potato gratin, broccoli rabe, and scotch ale sauce.

To make the sauce, melt the butter, beer, salt, and pepper together over medium heat, stirring constantly until the sauce become homogenous. Pour over meat and vegetables.

SWEET POTATO GRATIN

A wonderful twist on potato gratin, combining sweet potatoes, garlic, onions, and cream into a rich and comforting casserole.

Serves 8–12 people

5 pounds sweet potatoes, peeled and sliced

1^1/$_4$ cups olive oil

1 large white onion, thinly sliced

^{1}/$_2$ cup brown sugar

1 quart heavy cream

^{1}/$_4$ cup scotch ale

3 sprigs rosemary

1 teaspoon sea salt

1 teaspoon pepper

In a food processor, add rosemary, brown sugar, 1 cup olive oil, salt, and pepper. Mix until smooth and set aside. In the food processor, slice the sweet potatoes and onion in separate batches using a 2 mm blade. Toss them together, and sauté in ^{1}/$_4$ cup olive oil over high heat until a little color develops on the sweet potatoes. Add rosemary mixture to the potato mixture and gently mix. Return to the sauté pan and cook for 5 minutes, stirring often. Add ^{1}/$_2$ the cream and the beer, cook for 4 minutes, stirring often.

Add the rest of the cream and layer the potatoes into a 9"x11" pan. Cover with foil and bake in a 350 degree oven until sweet potatoes are tender, about 35 minutes. For best results, make the day before and reheat. This helps the flavors develop and the gratin hold together better.

SAUTÉED BROCCOLI RABE

Broccoli rabe is a vegetable that we believe deserves more credit. It is green, crunchy and pairs well with just about any entrée.

Serves 6–8 people

2 pounds broccoli rabe, cleaned and trimmed

3 tablespoons kosher salt

3 tablespoons olive oil

Sea salt and pepper to taste

Bring a large pot of water to a boil; add the kosher salt and broccoli rabe. Boil uncovered until it reaches al dente, about 3–5 minutes. When cooked drain and shock in an ice bath. Reheat the broccoli rabe in a sauté pan with the oil until hot, season to taste.

LEMONY BAKED ALASKA

This is one of my favorite pairings in the book. The 1809 Berliner Weisse ice cream is surprising and totally unique, and is finished with a fluffy burnt meringue and shortbread cookie.

Makes one 9 inch cake

8 lemons, zested and juiced
4 cups heavy cream
1$\frac{1}{2}$ cups sugar
8 egg yolks
$\frac{1}{2}$ cup Berliner Weisse beer
9 inch lemon sugar cookie
6 egg whites
1$\frac{1}{4}$ cups sugar

Combine 4 cups heavy cream and lemon zest in a medium saucepan. Bring mixture just to a simmer and remove from heat. Let sit for 10 minutes to infuse the lemon flavor into the cream. Bring to a simmer again.

In a separate medium bowl, whisk the egg yolks and the sugar until all combined. Gradually temper the warm cream mixture into the egg mix by adding the warm cream one ladle at a time, whisking constantly until all cream is combined with eggs. Return to the pot and cook over medium heat, stirring constantly, until it becomes thick enough to coat the back of a wooden spoon, about 3 to 5 minutes. Strain ice cream base through a fine chinois into a medium bowl set over a bowl of ice. Allow to cool, stirring occasionally.

When ice cream base is cool, stir in the lemon juice and beer. Process the base in an ice cream maker according to manufacturer›s instructions. Store in airtight container in your freezer.

When ice cream is finished freezing in the maker, assemble your Baked Alaska. Line a medium bowl with plastic wrap; being sure that the plastic is hanging over the sides of the bowl. Pour the ice cream in the bowl, smooth evenly, and place the shortbread on top, pressing down to secure it. Place in freezer until frozen solid. When the ice cream is frozen solid, warm the outside of the bowl slightly to remove. Place the ice cream cake on a platter cookie side down. Return to the freezer and make the meringue.

To make the meringue, mix the egg whites in a mixer on high speed with a whisk. Mix until the whites double in size and begin to get fluffy. Turn the mixer down to medium speed and slowly stream the sugar into the egg whites. When all the sugar is incorporated, turn the mixer up to high speed again and whisk until the whites reach a stiff peak. Place the whites in a piping bag with a star tip.

Remove the ice cream cake from the freezer and pipe the meringue all over the cake, being sure to cover the entire cake. Return to freezer until ready to serve.

When ready to serve the cake, remove it from the freezer 15 minutes early and let it warm up slightly. Use a kitchen torch to toast the meringue to golden brown all over the cake. (If you don't have a torch, place the frozen cake directly from the freezer under the broiler on high heat until topping is browned.) When the topping is nicely browned, slice and serve with a fruit coulis.

Note: you may also make individual Baked Alaskas using the same method above, simply choose a smaller mold.

RED CURRANT COULIS

This sauce is a perfect accompaniment to ice cream, lemon desserts, and even pancakes. We have chosen red currants for this sauce, but you could substitute another tart berry like raspberries, blackberries, or black currants.

Makes 1 cup

2 cups red currants or other berry
1/4 cup Berliner Weisse beer
1/2 cup water
1/2 cup sugar

Pick the berries off the stems and place them in a small saucepot with the beer, water, and sugar. Stir. Cook the berries over medium heat for about 10–12 minutes or until the berries become soft and falling apart and the sugar is completely dissolved.

Remove from the heat and let cool slightly. Pour the berry mix into a blender and blend until completely smooth. Pour the mix into a small bowl and cool completely in the refrigerator. This sauce can be made and stored for up to 2 weeks in the refrigerator.

SOFT LEMON SUGAR COOKIE

A tasty basic lemon cookie. Bake and ice with a light lemon glaze for an afternoon snack, or form the dough into an extra big cookie to use as a base for our Baked Alaska.

Makes about 3 dozen cookies

8 ounces unsalted butter, softened

2 cups sugar

2 tablespoons Berliner Weisse

2 lemons, zested and juiced

3 whole eggs

4 cups all-purpose flour

1 teaspoon baking powder

$1/2$ teaspoon sea salt

In a mixer combine the butter, sugar, lemon zest, and beer. Cream these ingredients with the paddle attachment on medium-high speed until the butter mix is fluffy. Add the eggs into the mix one at a time on medium speed until they are all combined; add the lemon juice from the 2 lemons, and mix. Stop the mixer and add the flour, baking powder, and salt. Start the mixer on slow and slowly increase the speed to medium as the flour becomes incorporated. Mix until it becomes a smooth dough. Remove from the bowl, wrap the dough in plastic wrap, and refrigerate for at least one hour.

When ready to use, remove from the refrigerator and roll out to desired shape and size. Bake cookies at 350 degrees for about 15 minutes or until light golden.

If you are using this recipe for the Baked Alaska, roll the dough out on a floured surface to $1/2$ inch thickness, cut the dough the same size and shape as the bowl you will be using for the Baked Alaska. Place on a cookie sheet and bake about 15 minutes or until light golden, be sure not to over bake to keep it soft. Cool and use as base for Baked Alaska.

NEW YEAR'S EVE

....

A dark, cold star-filled sky, the moon reflecting on hard snow, and a warm room filled with your most dear friends and family. Your best French beers flow freely and a light melody playing in the back ground. Who needs champagne on a night like this?

This menu combines the best of winter, from freshly shucked oysters to scallops and lamb, all followed by light puffs of custardy goodness—all paired with amazing beers that will immerse your party in good cheer, memories of the past year, and the resolutions for the new year.

So ring in the New Year with the best of everything, and the goodness, love, and passion that this meal represents. Cheers!!!

NEW YEAR'S EVE MENU
1st Course

    Oysters with cider mignonette

    Cidre Dupont Reserve, Domaine Familial Louis Dupont, France

2nd Course

    Pan Seared Scallops with crushed artichoke hearts, spinach, cauliflower puree, crunchy potatoes

    Les Biere Des Sans Culottes, Brasserie La Choulette, France

3rd Course

    Stuffed Lamb leg with herb stuffing, roasted root vegetables, demi-glace

    La Bavaissienne Ambree, Brasserie Theillier, France

4th Course

    Chocolate Milk Stout Cream Puffs with milk stout filling

    Milk Stout, Mikkeller ApS, Denmark

FEATURED BEERS

CIDRE DUPONT RESERVE
Made by: Domaine Familial Louis Dupont
Style: Cider
From: Victot-Pontfol, France
7% ABV
Serve in flute or lager glass

This natural cider has matured six months in oak casks which had previously contained calvados and has been bottled at the Domaine Dupont 14430 Victot-Pontfol France. ABV Varies year to year.

LES BIÈRE DES SANS CULOTTES
Made by: Brasserie La Choulette
Style: Bière de Garde
From: France
7% ABV
Serve in Flute

This beer pours a clear straw color and tastes of malty, caramel notes with lasting bitterness and tart fruit. This beer pairs well with seafood, poultry, fragrant cheeses, and stuffing.

LA BAVAISSIENNE AMBRÉE
Made by: Brasserie Theillier
Style: Bière de Garde
From: Bavay, France
7% ABV
Serve in snifter or tulip glass

In the little town of Bavay, only a few miles from the border with Belgium, the Theillier family has crafted its fine bière de garde for generations. The charming brewery is built into the Theillier family home, which was constructed in the 1600s on sturdy Roman foundations. La Bavaisienne is artfully brewed, in very small batches, using a resourceful combination of ancient and modern equipment.

MILK STOUT
Made by: Mikkeller ApS
Style: Milk Stout
From: Denmark
6% ABV
Serve in English pint

This beer pours black with a lasting tan head and tastes of mildly sweet cocoa, dark roasted coffee bitterness with a creamy vanilla finish. This beer pairs well with chocolate, vanilla, and coffee desserts, roasted foods, and barbecue.

RECIPES

CIDER MIGNONETTE SAUCE FOR OYSTERS

This sauce is the perfect pairing for fresh oysters on the half shell. The acidity complements the brininess of the oysters perfectly.

Makes ¹/₂ cup

1 tablespoon shallot, minced

2 tablespoons cider vinegar

¹/₂ cup cider

¹/₈ teaspoon sugar

¹/₈ teaspoon sea salt

¹/₈ teaspoon fresh ground black pepper

Peel and coarsely chop the shallots. Put them into a food processor and pulse a few times, until the shallots are finely minced, but not mushy. Combine the minced shallots, vinegar, cider, sugar, salt, and pepper into a small bowl. Chill until ready to serve. This sauce can be held for up to a month in the refrigerator.

PAN SEARED SCALLOPS WITH CRUSHED ARTICHOKE HEARTS, SPINACH, CAULIFLOWER PUREE, AND CRUNCHY POTATOES

This dish is one of our all-time favorites. The cauliflower puree is light and creamy, the scallops are perfectly tender and seared, and the crunch of the potatoes combined with the crushed artichoke hearts makes for a perfectly balanced dish. This dish works well as an entrée or can be made smaller for a perfect starter.

Serves 4 people

12 sea scallops
4 tablespoons olive oil
2 tablespoons butter
1 cup artichoke hearts
4 cups raw baby spinach
1 shallot, thinly sliced
6 tablespoons beer
4 tablespoons butter
Salt and pepper to taste
12 ounces cauliflower puree
12 ounces crunchy potatoes

Dry the scallops and remove the side mussel. Sprinkle scallops with salt and pepper. Put 4 tablespoons of oil in a large, flat-bottomed sauté pan, heat the oil until smoke point. Lay scallops in the pan flat side down, cook for 1–2 minutes and then flip and cook for another 1–2 minutes. Remove from the pan and set aside.

In a hot sauté pan add 2 tablespoons of butter and shallot, sauté for 20 seconds and add crushed artichoke hearts, spinach, salt, and pepper. Sauté until spinach is wilted. Deglaze the pan with 4 tablespoons beer.

Put this dish together by placing scallops, cauliflower puree, sautéed artichoke hearts, spinach, and crunchy potatoes on the plate. Finish dish by melting 4 tablespoons butter in a small pan, add 2 tablespoons beer on high heat, stirring continuously until it becomes homogeneous. Remove from heat and drizzle over the scallops.

CAULIFLOWER PUREE

Cauliflower puree is a great substitute for starchy dishes like potatoes. Use this recipe as a side for pretty much anything. This puree pairs well with scallops, duck, and chicken.

Serves 6 people
1 head cauliflower, cut into small pieces
1 small yellow onion, medium dice
2 cloves garlic
2 teaspoons sea salt
1 teaspoon pepper
$^1/_2$ cup heavy cream, warm
$^1/_2$ cup unsalted butter, melted

Bring 6 cups of water and 1 teaspoon of salt to a boil. Add the cauliflower, onion, and garlic. Boil the vegetables until they are tender, about 10–12 minutes. When vegetables are cooked strain them and place them in a blender, pulse the vegetables and add the cream, butter, salt, and pepper. Puree the mix until completely smooth, serve while hot.

CRUNCHY POTATOES

This recipe can be made with any small potato, but we prefer fingerling potatoes.

Serves 4–6 people

1 pound fingerling potatoes
1 tablespoon salt
2 cups vegetable oil
Salt and pepper to taste

Fill a large pot with ½ gallon of water and 1 tablespoon salt. Place potatoes in water and bring to a boil, covered. Cook until potatoes are tender, about 30 minutes. When potatoes are cooked, drain them and cool. Slice the potatoes in ½ inch slices.

Heat 2 cups oil to 340 degrees and fry potato slices until golden brown and crunchy about 4–5 minutes. Remove from oil and drain on paper towel. Salt and pepper to taste.

STUFFED LAMB LEG

A show stopper! Combine lamb, stuffing, roasted vegetables, and a strong ale demi-glace. This dish is as delicious as it is impressive.

Serves 8 people

1 leg of lamb, about 3–4 pounds, trimmed and boned

4 ounces white onion, small dice

2 ounces carrots, small dice

2 ounces celery, small dice

1 tablespoon unsalted butter

2 ounces smoked pepper bacon, finely chopped

3 shallots, chopped

4 tablespoons parsley, chopped

4 tablespoons rosemary, chopped

1 sprig of thyme

3 pinches fresh ground nutmeg

1 ounce white bread, crust removed

2 cloves garlic

1 teaspoon olive oil

Salt and pepper to taste

Melt the butter in saucepan over medium heat, cook the bacon in the butter for about 2 minutes and add the shallots, cover and cook for 2 minutes. Add carrots, onions, celery, parsley, rosemary, thyme, salt, pepper, nutmeg, and garlic, cook all together until carrots are tender. Add the bread crumbs to the mix. Set aside.

Preheat oven to 450 degrees. Stuff the lamb with the stuffing and tie together with string. Cook for 15 minutes then drop oven temperature to 375 degrees until internal temperature reaches 125–130 degrees. Remove from the oven and let rest. Slice the lamb and serve with roasted root vegetables and demi-glace.

VEAL DEMI-GLACE

This is the ultimate culinary sauce. It complements most meat dishes and is the base for our Shrimp and Grits.

Makes 2 cups

8 pounds veal bones
2 cups tomato paste
8 cups white onion, medium dice
4 cups celery, medium dice
4 cups carrots, medium dice
2¹/₄ cups red wine
2 tablespoons beer
Salt and pepper to taste

Place 8 pounds veal bones on sheet tray and coat the bones with the tomato paste. Bake in a 450 degree oven until golden brown about 35–45 minutes. When cooked place the bones in a large stockpot.

Take the sheet tray and place over an open flame and deglaze the pan with ¹/₄ cup red wine, scrape the bottom of the pan and pour this into the large stockpot. Add the vegetables to the stockpot and then fill the pots with cold water. Cover the pot and bring to a boil, reduce and simmer until it reduced by half. Strain through a fine mesh strainer and return the liquid to the stockpot, add 2 cups of red wine and reduce to 2 cups. Salt and pepper to taste and finish with the beer.

This sauce can be made ahead of time and can be stored in the refrigerator for up to 2 weeks. A great tip to have demi-glace on hand at all times is to freeze demi-glace in ice cube trays, pop them out when frozen and store in an airtight bag. They will last for 6 months in the freezer and can be de-thawed in minutes when needed.

ROASTED ROOT VEGETABLES

A warm, hearty winter side dish.

Serves 8 people

8 red bliss potatoes, cooked and cut in wedges

4 large carrots, peeled and cut into sticks

4 large parsnips, peeled and cut into sticks

2 large turnips, cleaned and cut into wedges

1/4 cup olive oil

2 sprigs rosemary

1 clove garlic, minced

Salt and pepper to taste

Start by cooking the potatoes. To make the potatoes, place them in cold salted water and cook them until tender about 20 minutes. Drain in a colander and cool the potatoes. When the potatoes are cool cut into wedges and toss with the oil, rosemary, garlic, salt, and pepper, carrots, parsnips, and turnips. Bake the carrots, parsnips, and turnips on sheet tray in a 450 degree oven for about 10 minutes, then add the potatoes and cook for another 10 minutes or until all the vegetables are golden brown and tender.

CHOCOLATE MILK STOUT CREAM PUFFS

This is a delicious and easy dessert to make. Impress your friends with this delicate mouthful of creamy milk stout and custard.

Makes about 12 cream puffs
Filling-
1 cup whole milk
5 tablespoons sugar
2 tablespoons cornstarch
$^1/_4$ teaspoon sea salt
4 large egg yolks
2 tablespoons unsalted butter
3 tablespoons milk stout
1 teaspoon vanilla

Puff shell-
$^1/_3$ cup unsalted butter
$^2/_3$ cup water
1 teaspoon vanilla
Pinch of sea salt
1 tablespoon sugar
$^2/_3$ cup all-purpose flour
3 large eggs

To make the custard filling heat the milk in a heavy saucepan. Bring to a simmer over medium heat. Stir together the sugar, cornstarch, and salt; then stir them into the egg until smooth. When the milk comes to a boil, temper the milk into the egg mixture. Return the mixture to the saucepan, and slowly bring to a boil, stirring constantly so the eggs don't curdle or scorch on the bottom.

When the mixture comes to a boil and thickens, cook for 1 minute, and remove from the heat. Immediately pour the custard into a medium size bowl that is sitting on a large bowl of ice. Stir in the butter, beer, and vanilla, mixing until the butter is completely blended in. Stir occasionally and let cool, refrigerate until chilled before using.

Preheat oven to 425 degrees. Start with the puff shells, in a large pot, bring the water, butter, vanilla, sugar, and salt to a rolling boil. Stir in flour until the mixture forms a ball and pulls away from the edges of the pan. Transfer the dough to a large mixing bowl. Using a wooden spoon or stand mixer, beat in the eggs one at a time, mixing well after each.

Drop by tablespoonfuls onto an ungreased baking sheet. Bake for 20 to 25 minutes in the pre-heated oven, until golden brown. Centers should be dry. When the shells are cool, either split and fill them with the pudding mixture, or use a pastry bag to pipe the pudding into the shells.

MARDI GRAS BUFFET

Some events just call for beer and food pairings! Mardi Gras is certainly an epic example of this. Our Cajun roots run deep—with lots of Louisiana relatives and memories of epic parties. As a young chef, Luther lived and breathed the beautiful New Orleans atmosphere, and perfected his Cajun recipes.

Mardi Gras is a party—a big, fun, boisterous party that cannot be confined to only a few dishes and beers. That's why we have set this menu up a little differently than most of the others. Mardi Gras deserves everything we've got, so we have included all of our favorite Cajun-style dishes in this chapter.

There's no party like a Cajun party! These dishes represent our passion and respect for the region and its residents. Laissez le bon temps rouler!

MARDI GRAS MENU

APPETIZERS:
Fried Louisiana Oysters with Creole mustard
Gumbo with chicken, shrimp, crawfish, Andouille sausage, okra and white rice

MAIN COURSES:
Crawfish Etouffe—Cajun stew of crawfish tails, peppers, onions, garlic, and white rice
Chicken and Tasso Jambalaya with smoked ham, chicken, rice dish seasoned Cajun tomato sauce
Louisiana Shrimp and Crawfish Boil with steamed spicy corn, potatoes, Andouille sausage, cocktail sauce, lemon
Red Beans and Rice with Tasso ham and Andouille sausage
Dirty Rice with ground chicken giblets, onions, chicken broth, green pepper, garlic

DESSERT:
Fresh Beignets
King Cake with whipped custard

FEATURED BEERS

RESTORATION PALE ALE

Made by: Abita Brewing Company
Style: American Pale Ale
From: Louisiana
5.20% ABV
Serve in a pint glass

    This beer pours golden and has a rich body. It is mildly bitter and has a hint of citrus finish. This beer pairs well with spicy foods, fish, and cheese.

AMBER ALE

Made by: Abita Brewing Company
Style: Vienne Lager
From: Louisiana
4.5% ABV
Serve in a pint glass

    This beer pours a rich amber color. This is a smooth beer with a slight caramel flavor and malt. It pairs well with spicy foods, crawfish, and smoked meats.

JOCKAMO IPA

Made by: Abita Brewing Company
Style: American IPA
From: Louisiana
6.5% ABV
Serve in a pint glass

    This beer pours a copper color. It is intensely hopped and is balanced out perfectly with the sweet malt flavors. It pairs well with spicy foods, grilled meats, and cheese.

PURPLE HAZE

Made by: Abita Brewing Company
Style: Fruit Beer
From: Louisiana
4.2% ABV
Serve in a pint glass

    This raspberry lager pours a light purple color. The fresh raspberries that were added create a fruity, tart, and slightly sweet flavor. This beer pairs well with salads and fruit desserts.

MARDI GRAS BOCK

Made by: Abita Brewing Company
Style: Maibock
From: Louisiana
6.5% ABV
Serve in a pint glass

    This seasonal beer pours clear orange-copper color. It is very rich and has a primarily malty sweetness. This beer pairs well with gumbo, roasted meats, fried foods, and king cake.

TURBODOG

Made by: Abita Brewing Company
Style: English Brown Ale
From: Louisiana
5.6% ABV
Serve in a pint glass

    This dark brown ale tastes of smoke, coffee, a bit of chocolate, and roasted barley. It pairs well with braised meats, jambalaya, and chocolate.

BLACKENED VOODOO LAGER

Made by: Dixie Brewing Company
Style: Schwarzbier
From: Louisiana
5% ABV
Serve in a lager glass

    This beer pours a light brown color. It tastes of amaretto and dark fruits, and finishes with slight bitter flavor. Pairs beautifully with burgers, steak, and spicy foods.

AMERICAN LAGER

Made by: Dixie Brewing Company
Style: American Lager
From: Louisiana
4.6% ABV
Serve in a lager glass

    This beer pours a light straw color. The medium carbonation delivers a fruity sweet lager with a slight bitter aftertaste. It pairs perfectly with crawfish.

RECIPES

BEER MARINATED FRIED OYSTERS

These are always a crowd pleaser. Add a little tartar with a dot of habanera sauce to spice them up!

Make 18–20 Oysters
1$^1/_2$ pints oysters or fresh, shucked oysters (18 to 20)
1 cup beer
1 cup all-purpose flour
1 cup yellow cornmeal
4 tablespoons cornstarch
$^1/_2$ teaspoon salt
$^1/_4$ teaspoon pepper
6 cups vegetable oil

Drain or shuck the oysters and marinate them in beer for 1 hour. Heat a deep pan with the oil to 350 degrees. In a separate bowl, mix all the dry ingredients. Coat the oysters in the mixture and set the oysters aside for a few minutes spread out on a paper towel.

Cook the oysters in the hot oil for about 2 minutes or until golden brown. Be careful not to overcook, or they will become chewy. Serve warm with your favorite sauce or enjoy plain with a twist of lemon.

TARTAR SAUCE

This classic sauce is popularly paired with seafood. It really adds a nice creamy texture to the fried oysters, crab cakes, or fish and chips. The splash of beer adds a nice flavor bridge to the beer-marinated oysters.

Makes 2$^1/_2$ cups
2 cups mayonnaise
$^3/_4$ cup pickles, finely chopped
$^1/_4$ teaspoon sea salt
$^1/_4$ teaspoon black pepper, freshly ground
$^1/_4$ teaspoon Worcestershire Sauce
$^1/_4$ teaspoon cayenne pepper
1 teaspoon beer

Finely chop the pickles. Add the pickles, salt, pepper, Worcestershire sauce, cayenne pepper, and beer to the 2 cups of mayonnaise.

Mix all the ingredients until combined. Chill and serve. This recipe will last in the refrigerator for up to two weeks.

SEAFOOD GUMBO

This classic Cajun-Creole soup is chock full of chicken, seafood, and zesty sausage. Our family actually orders our own special andouille directly from Louisiana for this dish. Whenever we serve a bowl, we feel like we are back there.

Serves 8 people

1^1/$_2$ cups uncooked rice
2^1/$_2$ cups water
pinch salt and pepper
1 bay leaf

7 cups chicken stock
^{1}/$_2$ cup all-purpose flour
^{1}/$_2$ cup unsalted butter
1 cup white onions, finely diced
1 cup green bell peppers, finely diced
^{3}/$_4$ cup celery, finely diced
1 tablespoon fresh garlic, minced
2 tablespoons Cajun seasoning
1 pound chicken legs and thighs
^{1}/$_2$ pound Andouille sausage
1 pound shrimp, peeled and deveined
1 pound crawfish tails, shelled
2 tablespoons filé seasoning

Soak the rice for 10 minutes in hot water. This brief soaking help separates the grains and creates fluffier rice with less sticky starch. Drain and rinse the rice, and place it in medium saucepan with water, salt, pepper, and bay leaf. Cover and cook for about 12 minutes or until tender.

Bring the chicken stock to a boil and set it aside until you are ready to use.

Next, make the roux. The key to a perfect gumbo is a dark brown roux. To make this, heat the butter and flour in a medium saucepan over medium heat. It is essential that you stir constantly to prevent the flour from burning. Use a wooden spoon, being sure to scrape the bottom of the pan as you go. Keep stirring until the roux is dark red-brown.

When the roux is dark brown, add the onions, celery, peppers, garlic, and Cajun seasoning and stir until combined. Then add the chicken and Andouille and stir until combined. When the vegetables and meat is combined, slowly add the stock, 1 cup at a time, stirring until fully incorporated before adding the next cup. When all the stock has been added, turn the heat to low, and simmer for 35–40 minutes.

Before serving, add the shrimp and crawfish. Simmer for about 10 minutes. Finish with the filé seasoning and serve over hot rice.

CHICKEN AND TASSO JAMBALAYA

A hearty rice dish, chock full of rich sauce and your choice of meats. We include chicken and spicy ham here, but add a handful of shrimp, sausage, or ground meat if that suits your fancy.

Serves 4 people

1^1/$_2$ cups uncooked rice
2^1/$_2$ cups water
pinch salt and pepper
1 bay leaf

1^1/$_2$ cups tomato stock
8 large tomatoes
1 teaspoon salt
1 teaspoon pepper
2 cloves garlic
1 tablespoon Cajun seasoning
2 tablespoons olive oil
2 tablespoons unsalted butter
^{1}/$_2$ pound chopped Tasso, diced
^{3}/$_4$ pound boneless chicken, cut into bite-sized pieces
2 tablespoons Cajun seasoning
2 bay leaves
6 fresh sage leaves, chopped
1 cup onions, chopped
1 cup celery, chopped
1 cup green bell peppers, chopped
2 cloves fresh garlic, minced
2^1/$_2$ cups chicken stock

Soak the rice for 10 minutes in hot water. This brief soaking help separates the grains and creates fluffier rice with less sticky starch. Drain and rinse the rice, and place it in medium saucepan with water, salt, pepper, and bay leaf. Cover and cook for about 12 minutes or until tender. When rice is cooked. Remove it from the pan and spread on a sheet pan. Cool rice and store in refrigerator, uncovered overnight. (Chilling the rice dries it out slightly and makes it ready to soak up the sauces. Skip refrigeration if you are short on time.)

Make the tomato stock: roughly chop 8 tomatoes, and combine them with salt, pepper, garlic, Cajun seasoning, and olive oil in a large saucepan. Cook mixture covered over medium-low heat for about an hour. Remove cover and continue simmering until sauce reduces to about 1^1/$_2$ cups. Puree the mix and set aside.

Melt the butter in a 2-quart saucepan over high heat. Add the Tasso and cook, stirring frequently for about three minutes or until it begins to brown. Add the chicken and continue cooking until the chicken is browned, about 5 minutes. Stir in 2 tablespoons Cajun seasoning, 2 bay leaves, sage, ^{1}/$_2$ of the onions, celery, and bell peppers, and the garlic. Continue to cook the mixture, stirring continuously and scraping the pan bottom as needed, until the vegetables start to get tender, about 5 to 8 minutes. Stir in the tomato stock and cook for about a minute. Stir in the remaining onions, celery, bell peppers, and chicken stock. Bring to a boil then reduce heat to low. Cover and simmer about 18 minutes. In the last 2–3 minutes, stir in the cooled cooked rice. Heat until the rice is hot and the liquid absorbs into it. Let sit for about 5 minutes before serving.

LOUISIANA CRAWFISH BOIL

It's all here, so come and get it! Fresh steamed crawfish, spicy sausage, potatoes, and corn. A glorious one-pot meal, if ever there was one!

Serves 6 people

10 pounds live crawfish
8 cups lager beer
4 white onions, unpeeled
$1/4$ cup cayenne pepper
$1/2$ cup sea salt
2 tablespoons ground pepper
$1/2$ cup sugar
1 pound Andouille
12 small potatoes, unpeeled
2 garlic cloves, unpeeled
6 ears fresh corn, husked
$1/8$ cup Cajun seasoning

Begin by washing the crawfish, place them in a sink and rinse crawfish in cool water until clean. Remove and discard any dead crawfish, fill the sink with cold water to cover the crawfish until ready to cook.

Over high heat bring $2 1/2$ gallons of water and 8 cups of lager beer to a boil in a covered 6 gallon pot. When the water-beer mix is boiling, add the onions, garlic, cayenne pepper, salt, pepper, sugar, Andouille, and potatoes. Cook for 30 minutes. Add the corn on the cob and cook for 5 minutes or until corn is tender. Remove the corn, Andouille and potatoes. Drain the crawfish and add them to the pot and cook for 15 minutes. Remove everything from the pot and serve.

CRAWFISH ETOUFFEE

A classic Cajun crawfish dish with just a hint of spice. Etouffee means "smothered," in this case with a sauce using the Cajun Holy Trinity of onion, celery, and bell pepper. Substitute shrimp if you can't get fresh crawfish.

Serves 8 people

$1/4$ cup white onion, small dice

$1/4$ cup celery, small dice

$1/4$ cup green bell pepper, small dice

$1/2$ cup butter, unsalted

$3/4$ cup all-purpose flour

2 tablespoons Cajun seasoning

3 cups seafood stock

$1/2$ pound unsalted butter

$1/2$ cup beer

2 pounds crawfish, whole and uncooked

1 cup scallions, very finely diced

4 cups white rice, cooked

Peel the crawfish and use the shells to make the stock (vegetable stock may be used as a substitute).

Combine the onion, celery, and bell pepper in a bowl and set aside. Combine butter and flour in warm thick bottom pan (we prefer cast iron) to make the roux, stir continuously with a wooden spoon until a dark reddish brown color is achieved; this will take about 20 minutes. Be sure to keep stirring and scrapping the bottom to prevent any burning.

Remove from the heat and immediately stir in the vegetables and half the Cajun seasoning.

Bring 2 cups of the stock to a boil. Add the hot stock slowly to the roux and vegetable mix, stir until the roux is dissolved and completely incorporated to the stock. Reduce the heat to low and cook for 45 minutes, stirring occasionally. Remove from the heat and set aside.

Melt 1 stick of the butter in a large sauté saucepan over medium heat. When pan is hot, stir in the crawfish and the green onions, stirring constantly for about 1 minute. Add the remaining butter, the roux mixture, and the remaining seafood stock. Cook in the pan until the butter melts and is mixed into the sauce, about 4 to 6 minutes. Add the remaining Cajun seasoning, stir well, and remove from the heat. If the sauce starts to separate, add 2 tablespoons more stock or water and stir the pan until it combines. Serve immediately over the rice.

RED BEANS AND RICE

Traditionally cooked on Mondays to take advantage of Sunday's leftover ham, this dish could simmer nicely all day while the laundry and other household chores were being done. This is a simple dish, but one that satisfies to the bones after a busy day.

Serves 8 people
1 pound dry red kidney beans
2 tablespoons olive oil
2 cloves garlic, crushed
1 large white onion, medium dice
1 green bell pepper, medium dice
1 cup celery, medium dice
3/4 pound Tasso ham, medium dice
1 1/2 pounds Andouille
1 teaspoon fresh thyme
2 bay leaves
1 tablespoon Worcestershire sauce
2 tablespoons Cajun seasoning
1/2 tablespoon sea salt
1/2 tablespoon pepper
1/2 cup amber beer
3 1/2 cups water
8 cups cooked rice

Soak the beans in cold water overnight. When ready to make this dish, drain and rinse the beans. Set aside.

Heat a large sautepan and add the oil, garlic, onions, green pepper, and celery. Sauté vegetables until the onion is translucent. Add the Tasso ham and Andouille sausage and cook until brown and caramelized. Season with the thyme, bay leaves, Worcestershire sauce, Cajun seasoning, and salt and pepper. Sauté for 2 minutes.

Add the beans, water, and beer, stir until combined. Simmer over medium heat for 1 1/2–2 hours, stirring occasionally or until beans are cooked and tender. This dish improves with age, so make it in advance and reheat; the flavors will improve and come together. Serve with rice.

DIRTY RICE

At our house this is the ultimate side dish, although it is so hearty and full of meat, it can easily stand alone. Finish with raw egg and add a sprinkle of hot pepper vinegar to make it truly authentic.

Serves 6 people
2 tablespoons vegetable oil
$3/4$ pound ground chicken gizzards, hearts, and livers
$1/4$ pound ground pork
2 bay leaves
3 tablespoons Cajun seasoning
1 teaspoon dry mustard
1 teaspoon ground cumin
$1/2$ cup white onions, medium dice
$1/2$ cup celery, medium dice
$1/2$ cup green bell peppers, medium dice
2 teaspoons fresh garlic, minced
4 cups chicken stock
1 egg
1 cup uncooked rice
1 cup water
1 teaspoon sea salt
1 bay leave
4 whole peppercorns
1 pod cardamom

In a large, heavy skillet add the oil, heat for 1 minute, then add the chicken gizzards, hearts, livers, and ground pork. Cook until the meat is browned. Add the next 8 ingredients and cook until vegetables are browned. Add the stock to the pot and simmer covered for 2 hours. When 2 hours has passed, remove from heat and finely dice all the ingredients but the bay leaves in a food processor.

After the meat mix has been simmering for 30 minutes, begin cooking the rice. In a medium sauce pot combine 1 cup rice, 1 cup water, cardamom, peppercorns, salt, and bay leaves. Cook the rice over low, low heat, covered for $1^1/2$ hours. This method allows the rice to absorb the flavors more completely and creates a very tender rice.

When rice is cooked, combine in a medium bowl the finely diced meat mix and the rice, mix until all combined. Add the egg raw and stir until all combined. Serve.

BEIGNETS

These light puffs of fried goodness are synonymous with New Orleans. Serve with dark rich Cajun coffee or a rich malty pour of beer.

Makes 14 doughnuts

1 ounce active dry yeast
1 cup warm water
$^1/_3$ cup sugar
3 tablespoons milk
1 egg
1 teaspoon sea salt
$4^1/_2$ cups bread flour
6 cups vegetable oil
1 cup powdered sugar

Combine the yeast and warm water in a large bowl and set aside for 10 minutes. Add the sugar, milk, egg, salt, and flour to the dissolved yeast mix. Combine to form a soft dough ball and knead on a floured surface until smooth about 6 minutes. Let the dough rise for 1 hour by placing it in a greased bowl and covering it with a damp towel. Dough should double in size, keeping it in a warm spot will help the dough rise faster.

Preheat oil in a thick bottomed medium pan to 340 degrees. After dough has doubled in size, punch it down and roll out on a floured surface with a rolling pin to $^1/_4$ inch thickness and cup into 2x2 inch squares. When oil reaches the desired temperature carefully drop the 2x2 dough squares into the oil and fry until light brown and fluffy about 3 minutes. Remove from the oil and drain on paper towels. To serve roll the doughnuts in powdered sugar and eat hot.

KING CAKE

It's all about the baby. The tradition of king cake seems to have begun to celebrate Epiphany, the time when the Wise Men discovered the Christ Child. Somehow the timing has slid a bit, and now it is the traditional dessert of Mardi Gras. The finder of the plastic trinket usually is treated to some special privilege or gift.

Makes 1 King Cake

1 ounce active dry yeast

1 cup warm water

$^1/_3$ cup sugar

3 tablespoons milk

1 egg

1 teaspoon sea salt

$4^1/_2$ cups bread flour

1 cup brown sugar

1 tablespoon cinnamon

1 tablespoon nutmeg

1 teaspoon sea salt

$^1/_2$ cup flour

$^1/_2$ cup unsalted butter, melted

2 tablespoons stout beer

1 cup powdered sugar

2–3 tablespoons beer

Purple, green, and gold sprinkles

1 small plastic baby

Combine the yeast and warm water in a large bowl and set aside for 10 minutes. Add the sugar, milk, egg, salt, and flour to the dissolved yeast mix. Combine to form a soft dough ball and knead on a floured surface until smooth about 6 minutes. Let the dough rise for 1 hour by placing it in a greased bowl and covering it with a damp towel. Dough should double in size, keeping it in a warm spot will help the dough rise faster.

Combine the sugar, cinnamon, nutmeg, salt, flour, melted butter, and beer in a small bowl. Set aside.

After dough has doubled in size, punch it down and roll out on a floured surface with a rolling pin to $^1/_4$ inch thickness, be sure to roll the dough twice as long as it is wide. When dough is ready spread the sugar mix evenly over the entire dough. Roll the dough up like a jelly roll and make into a circle, attaching the two ends together. Put the cake in a warm place and let rise until it has doubled in size. Bake in a 375 degree oven for about 30 minutes or until golden brown. Let cool.

Combine the powdered sugar and beer in a small bowl and frost the cake after it is cool. Be sure you frost the entire top, sprinkle the colored sprinkles in rows on the cake and insert the baby in the bottom of the cake. Serve warm with whipped custard.

WHIPPED CUSTARD

This custard is light, creamy and goes with anything. We have paired it with the king cake.

Makes about 5 cups

$^1/_2$ cup beer
3 cups whole milk
2 teaspoons vanilla
$^3/_4$ cups sugar
Pinch of sea salt
6 egg yolks
$^1/_4$ cup corn starch
4 tablespoons unsalted butter
1 cup heavy cream
3 tablespoons powdered sugar

Bring the milk, beer, and vanilla to a simmer in a medium sauce pot. Combine the sugar, salt and corn starch in a medium bowl, add the egg yolks and whisk until the mix is completely smooth. Slowly whisk the hot milk into the egg mix until half the milk is incorporated with the eggs, then pour the milk-egg mix back into the sauce pot and return to the stove. Over high heat bring the mix to a boil, be sure to whisk the mix continuously as it thickens. Once mix is thick and boiling, let boil for 1 minute to cook the starch flavor out. Immediately pour the mix into a bowl and cool over an ice bath. While the custard is cooling add the butter. Let cool completely.

In a separate bowl whisk the heavy cream and powdered sugar until the cream reaches soft peaks. Fold the cool custard with the whipped cream and serve.

SPRING

SPRING MAKES ITS APPEARANCE WITH SOFTENING TEMPERATURES AND GENTLE SHOWERS, AND BRINGS ALONG WITH IT TENDER GREENS AND FIDDLEHEADS, FRESH PEAS AND SUCCULENT MOREL MUSHROOMS, ALONG WITH LAMB AND LOVELY COLD WEATHER SEAFOOD. OUR BEER CHOICES ARE STILL HEARTY, BUT WE START TO MAKE ROOM FOR THE LIGHTER LAGERS AND ALES OF WARMER WEATHER.

ST. PATRICK'S DAY

On St. Patrick's Day, everyone claims a touch of the Irish. This day has a long history in America, and has turned a saint's feast day into quite a party. Our pub is hopping on this night, and we make the most of it, pairing the amazing food inspired by the Irish with some of our favorite beer. So gather your friends and come on by! And if you can't, then try some of these great recipes and pairings for yourself at home.

ST. PATRICK'S DAY MENU

1st Course:
    Fried Darú Irish Cheese, with watercress, arugula, yellow beets, cucumbers, cherry tomatoes, Harp Lager dressing, and Soda Bread
    Harp Lager, Guinness Ltd, Ireland
2nd Course:
    Corned Beef and Cabbage
    Smithwick's Irish Ale, Guinness Ltd, Ireland
3rd Course:
    Chocolate Guinness Pie with malted whipped cream
    Guinness Foreign Extra, Guinness Ltd, Ireland

FEATURED BEERS

HARP LAGER
Made by: Guinness Ltd/ Diaego
Style: Pale Lager
From: Ireland
5% ABV
Serve in a Lager glass

This beer pours dark golden in color and is a well balanced beer brewed on the lighter side it is crisp and dry with a malty, hoppy base. This beer pairs well with lighter fare, salads, and sandwiches.

SMITHWICK'S IRISH ALE
Made by: Guinness Ltd
Style: Irish Ale
From: Ireland
4.5% ABV
Serve in a English Pint

This beer pours a clear red copper color. This is a balanced beer with some sweet malt, light citrus, and a woody bitterness flavor. This beer pairs with sausage, mashed potatoes, corned beef and cabbage, and fried foods.

GUINNESS FOREIGN EXTRA
Made by: Guinness Ltd
Style: Stout
From: Ireland
7.5% ABV
Serve in an English Pint

This beer pours black with a creamy tan head. It tastes of coffee, burnt sugar, chocolate, and sweet malts. It finishes with a nice bitter flavor that balances it all out. This beer pairs well with desserts and braised meats.

RECIPES

IRISH WATERCRESS SALAD WITH FRIED DARU IRISH CHEESE

This is a traditional Irish salad with our twist. We have paired it with a creamy harp dressing and soda bread, a nice light start to any meal.

Serves 4 people
4 ounces Daru Irish cheese
2 whole eggs
pinch salt and pepper
1/2 cup all-purpose flour
1/2 cup panko bread crumbs
3 cups watercress
3 cups arugula
2 whole eggs, hard boiled
1 large red beet, cleaned and boiled
1 large cucumber
12 cherry tomatoes, halved
2 cups olive oil

Divide the cheese into 1 ounce pieces. Whisk 2 eggs, salt, and pepper in a small bowl and put the flour and bread crumbs in separate small bowls. Dip the cheese into the egg mix, then the flour, dip the cheese back into the egg mix, and then coat with the bread crumbs. Refrigerate for 10 minutes.

Clean and dry the watercress and arugula and put in a medium sized bowl. Remove the hard-boiled egg yolks from the egg whites; reserve the yolks for the dressing. Chop the egg whites in small pieces and add to the water-cress mix. Chop the cleaned and cooked beet into small pieces and add to the watercress mix. Peel and chop the cucumber in small pieces and add to salad mix with the halved cherry tomatoes.

Heat the oil in a medium pot to 350 degrees. Carefully place the cheese in the hot oil and cook for about 2 minutes or until golden brown, remove and let rest a few minutes.

Mix the salad and divide it by 4. Serve with the fried cheese and harp dressing on the side.

HARP LAGER DRESSING

This dressing is a twist on a traditional Irish dressing; we have paired it with the Watercress Salad.

Makes 1/2 cup
2 hardboiled egg yolks
1/4 cup Dijon mustard
1/2 teaspoon sea salt
1/2 teaspoon ground pepper
1 tablespoon brown sugar
1 tablespoon cider vinegar
1 teaspoon olive oil
1 tablespoon lager
4 tablespoons heavy cream

Combine the egg yolks, mustard, sugar, salt, and pepper in a blender. Blend until the ingredients are smooth. Slowly add the vinegar, beer, and oil until all combined. Add the cream and mix until just combined, do not over mix. Serve with your favorite salad.

CORNED BEEF BRISKET WITH CABBAGE, ONIONS, AND POTATOES

Corned beef has a long history in America and has traditionally been served by Irish Americans for St. Patrick's Day. This is not a fancy meal, but it certainly is a satisfying one.

Serves 6–8 people
1¹/₂ gallons boiling water
1¹/₂ tablespoons whole cloves
1 tablespoon fresh ginger, minced
2 stick whole cinnamon
1 tablespoon dry mustard
¹/₂ cup fresh ground black pepper
5 bay leaves
2 pounds kosher salt
8 cups Irish cream beer

1 large beef brisket
12–16 small Irish potatoes
3 tablespoons kosher salt
1 large green cabbage, large dice
2 medium white onions, large dice
¹/₂ cup bacon fat, cook ¹/₂ pound bacon—save fat
¹/₄ cup Irish cream beer
Salt and pepper to taste

Bring the first 8 ingredients to boil. Place the beef and 8 cups of beer in a large pot and cover the beef with hot brine mixture, make sure beef is fully submerged, and then weigh it down with plate. Let the beef sit in the brine in the refrigerator for about 1–2 weeks.

Put the potatoes in a large pot, cover them with water and add the salt. Simmer until they are cooked about 30 minutes. Set aside.

After the meat has sat in the brine for a week or two, remove it and wash the meat in cold water to remove the extra brine. Combine the first 7 ingredients in a large pot and submerge the beef and simmer until tender about 4–5 hours. Remove the meat and let rest. When ready to eat, slice the beef against the grain.

In a cold sauté pan add the cabbage, bacon fat, and onions. Heat the cabbage and onions over medium heat with a tight lid. Sweat the cabbage and onions until they become translucent, but have no caramel color. Add the beer, salt, and pepper, simmer for 2 minutes.

Serve the corned beef on a bed of the cabbage and onion mix and boiled potatoes.

IRISH SODA BREAD

This is a classic soda bread recipe, especially good with plenty of honey butter.

Makes 1 loaf

$^1/_4$ cup Irish cream beer

3 tablespoons sugar

4 cups bread flour

1 teaspoon baking soda

1 tablespoon baking powder

$^1/_2$ teaspoon sea salt

$^1/_2$ teaspoon ground black pepper

4 ounces unsalted butter, softened

1 cup, 1 tablespoon buttermilk

1 whole egg

Preheat the oven to 375 degrees. In a small pot combine the beer and sugar, bring to a boil for 1 minute. Remove from heat and chill completely. Then combine the flour, baking soda, baking powder, salt, and pepper in a large bowl. Combine the cooled beer mix with the buttermilk and pour into the dry ingredients. Add the softened butter and egg. Mix until dough forms. Pour the dough onto a lightly floured surface and knead to form a ball, do not over work. Place the dough on a greased baking pan and cut a cross on the top of the dough. Brush the dough with 1 tablespoon of buttermilk and sprinkle with salt. Bake the bread for about 40–50 minutes. Check doneness with a toothpick, which will come out clean when done.

PIE DOUGH

This basic pie dough recipe will work for all of your sweet pies. For a more savory crust, omit the vanilla and sugar.

Makes two 9-inch inch pie shells

2 cups all-purpose flour

2 tablespoons sugar

1 teaspoon kosher salt

1 cup unsalted butter, cold

$^1/_2$ cup water

1 tablespoon vanilla

Place the flour, sugar, and salt in a medium bowl and mix. Cut the cold butter into small pieces and place in the flour mix. Mix the butter into the flour mix until the butter is in pea size pieces and mix is a little crumbly. Add the water and vanilla and mix until dough comes together. Be careful to not over mix; this will create a tough dough. Refrigerate for at least 1 hour. Separate your dough into 2 equal pieces, reserve 1 half for another pie (unless you are making a double crusted pie) the dough freezes beautifully. Roll the dough out on a floured surface to fit your desired pie dish. Refrigerate while you prepare the filling.

GUINNESS PIE

A favorite at our restaurant. We have requests year-round for this sweet Guinness pie, but we always love to share it during our St. Patrick's celebrations.

Makes one 9-inch pie
1 deep, 9-inch pie shell
2$\frac{1}{2}$ ounces unsalted butter
$\frac{3}{4}$ cup light corn syrup
1 tablespoon vanilla
$\frac{1}{2}$ cup Guinness beer
$\frac{2}{3}$ cup sugar
$\frac{1}{4}$ cup cocoa powder
4 whole eggs

$\frac{2}{3}$ cup sugar
1 cup heavy whipping cream
2 tablespoons Guinness beer
1 teaspoon vanilla
1 tablespoon cocoa powder
$\frac{1}{4}$ cup powdered sugar

Preheat the oven to 350 degrees. Combine the butter, corn syrup, vanilla, and beer in a medium pot; begin cooking over high heat. In a separate small bowl combine $\frac{2}{3}$ cup sugar and cocoa powder and whisk these ingredients into the corn syrup mix. Bring the mix to a boil. Whisk the eggs and $\frac{2}{3}$ cup sugar in a medium size bowl. Temper the hot corn syrup mix into the eggs and sugar, slowly adding hot mix while whisking constantly. When the mix is all combined, pour it into the pie shell and bake for about 45 minutes or until the center of the pie is no longer wobbly. Chill.

To make the whipped cream, combine the heavy whipping cream, 2 tablespoons beer, 1 teaspoon vanilla, 1 tablespoon cocoa powder, and $\frac{1}{4}$ cup of powdered sugar in a mixing bowl with the whisk attachment. Whisk until the mix becomes thick and can hold a soft peak. Do not over mix; it will become grainy and will separate. Serve on top of the Guinness Pie.

SPRING SUPPER

Charlottesville is a wonderland of small farms. And when we buy locally, we find that the local lamb, goat cheese, herbs, and vegetables just taste a little sweeter.

This is one of our family's favorite Sunday meals, especially for our young son. We love the marinated lamb chops, fresh sautéed fiddleheads and ramps, the fresh herb salad, and an easy-to-bake carrot cupcake to end the meal.

Craft beer and food are made for each other and this chapter really brings it all together.

The Double Trouble Imperial IPA makes a fantastic vinaigrette with the citrus notes. The Troubadour Obscura compliments the veal-demi glace and lamb, perfectly adding an extra depth of flavor to an already luscious sauce. The hazelnut carrot cupcakes are also made better with an amazing Hazelnut Brown Nectar by Rogue.

SPRING SUPPER MENU
1st Course
    Fried Fig-Stuffed Goat Cheese, herb salad, Double Trouble Vinaigrette
    Double Trouble Imperial IPA, Founders Brewing Company, Michigan
2nd Course
    Roasted French Lamb Chops with sautéed roasted potatoes, ramps, fiddleheads, morels and lamb demi-glace
    Troubadour Obscura Mild Stout, Brouwerij De Musketier, Belgium
3rd Course
    Hazelnut Carrot Cake Cupcakes with Hazelnut Brown Ale cream cheese frosting
    Hazelnut Brown Nectar, Rogue Ales, Oregon

FEATURED BEERS

DOUBLE TROUBLE IMPERIAL IPA
Made by: Founders Brewing Company
Style: Imperial IPA
From: Michigan
9.4% ABV
Serve in a Pint glass
    This beer pours dark burnt-orange with a nice silky head. The taste is of strong bitter hops surrounded by strong pine flavor, lemon, and grapefruit balanced with light honey and malts. This beer pairs well with salads, citrus desserts, cream.

TROUBADOUR OBSCURA MILD STOUT
Made by: Brouwerij De Musketier
Style: Mild Stout
From: Belgium
8.5% ABV
Serve in a Trappist Glass
    This beer pours dark red-brown with a dense, creamy head. This is a good complex Belgian beer. The flavor has sour bites which are followed by strong dark fruit, light black licorice, and caramel. Faint citrus notes rounded out with big, robust coffee, and nutty chestnut notes. This beer pairs well with demi-glace, grilled red meats, roasted meats.

HAZELNUT BROWN NECTAR
Made by: Rogue Ales
Style: American Brown Ale
From: Oregon
6.2% ABV
Serve in a Dimpled Mug
     This beer pours dark brown in color and the taste is creamy, roasted nuts, toffee, and malt. This beer pairs well with nuts, cream, deserts, and pork.

RECIPES

HERB SALAD WITH FRIED FIG-STUFFED GOAT CHEESE BALLS

This salad is so full of flavor. It is so fresh and light, with every bite singing a new note of basil, parsley, mint, spring onions, and arugula. When you add the contrast of fig and soft, warm goat cheese, you have a definite crowd pleaser.

Serves 4 people
6 ounces fig paste or fresh figs
12 ounces goat cheese, softened
2 tablespoons extra virgin olive oil
1 teaspoon sea salt
1 teaspoon fresh ground black pepper
12 ounces all-purpose flour
4 whole eggs
12 ounces panko bread crumbs

2 quarts vegetable oil for frying
1 ounce arugula
1 ounce chives
1 ounce basil
1 ounce flat leaf parsley
1 ounce mint
1 ounce tarragon
1 ounce garlic chives
$1/2$ ounce rosemary
$1/2$ ounce pansy edible flowers, optional

First make the goat cheese balls. Allow the goat cheese to come to room temperature. Mix salt, pepper, and olive oil into the goat cheese and set aside. Shape the fig paste into $1/2$ ounce balls and mold 1 ounce goat cheese mix around the fig balls to about a $1/4$ inch thickness, refrigerate for 10 minutes. Crack eggs in separate bowl and whisk them. Set up 3 separate bowls in a row, 1 with the eggs, 1 with flour, 1 with bread crumbs. Bread all the goat cheese balls—dip the goat cheese balls in eggs, flour, eggs, and bread crumbs. Chill the breaded cheese for at least 1 hour; these can be made in advance.

Fill a deep, very heavy skillet for frying with the vegetable oil. Leave at least 2 inches of space at the top to prevent overflow once food is added. Preheat oil to 350 degrees. Once oil has reached the desired temperature, place the goat cheese balls in the oil and cook for approximately $2 1/2$ minutes or until golden brown. Remove from the oil, drain on paper towels, and set aside.

Next you will assemble you herbs and lettuce. Clean all herbs in cold water and pat the herbs dry. Fine chop the rosemary and put it in a medium size bowl. Cut larger leaves to bite size pieces, otherwise leave leaves whole. Mix all herbs and arugula together and toss with dressing. Garnish with pansy edible flowers.

FOUNDER'S DOUBLE TROUBLE VINAIGRETTE

The really great thing about this dressing is how versatile it is. Use it for marinating or salads, and feel free to experiment with different types of Beer—it works with almost any kind.

Makes 1¹/₂ cups

1 cup extra virgin olive oil
¹/₂ cup Founder's Double Trouble beer
1 each shallot peeled
1 each garlic cloves, peeled
2 each sprigs parsley, leaves removed from stem
1 teaspoon salt
1 teaspoon black pepper

Combine all ingredients in a blender except the oil. Blend the ingredients until completely combined and chopped up. Add the oil in a steady stream until all are incorporated. Serve on salad. May be stored for up to 1 week.

SAUTÉED RAMPS, FIDDLEHEADS, AND MORELS

This dish says pure springtime, and is one of the rare recipes that simply cannot be made out of season. It is well worth the extra effort to find these wonderful tender vegetables. Pair with lamb or fresh fish.

Serves 4 people
1/2 pound ramps
1/2 pound fiddlehead ferns
1/2 pound morels
4 tablespoons butter
Sea salt to taste
Fresh ground black pepper to taste

Clean the ramps thoroughly, trim off the tough stalk ends and slice the ramps thinly. Clean the fiddleheads thoroughly and gently dry them with a paper towel. Clean the morels with a dry cloth, brushing the dirt off. In a hot sauté pan add the butter, lightly brown it and add the ramps, sauté them until they are translucent. Add the morels and sauté about 30 seconds. Add the fiddleheads and sauté another 30 seconds, season to taste.

ROASTED FRENCH LAMB CHOPS AND LAMB DEMI-GLACE WITH TROUBADOUR OBSCURA MILD STOUT

Lamb chops are our family's favorite meal; we marinate them in a rosemary dressing and give them a quick grill. The sides we serve with them changes seasonally, but in the spring we love to pair them with sautéed roasted potatoes, ramps, fiddleheads, and morels.

Serves 4 people
1 cup extra virgin olive oil
6 cloves garlic
10 sprigs rosemary
1 tablespoon sea salt
2 teaspoons fresh ground black pepper
8 each fingerling potatoes or 8 small red bliss potatoes
2 racks French Lamb chops, cleaned and cut apart

Puree rosemary, garlic, salt, and pepper with olive oil in blender until all combined. Split the marinade in half, reserve half for the potatoes, and half for the lamb. Wash the potatoes and place them in salted cold water. Cover the potatoes and bring them to a boil. Cook until the potatoes are cooked; this will take about 20 minutes. When cooked, drain and cool. When potatoes are cool cut them into the desired size and toss the potatoes with marinade. Place them on a cookie sheet and cook until golden brown in preheated 450 degree oven for about 10 minutes.

There are 2 ways you could cook and serve your lamb chops. If you prefer to embrace the gamey quality of the Lamb we suggest that you leave the lamb rack whole. If you prefer your lamb to be less gamey we suggest you prepare your lamb as pre-cut chops.

The first way to cook the lamb chops is whole lamb chops. Pour half the marinade over lamb chops and marinate for about 30–45 minutes or up to overnight. Place lamb rack on sheet tray fat side down in 350 degree oven. Cook the lamb roast until desired temperature is reached. Our suggested temperature is medium-rare.

The second way to cook them is to grill pre-cut lamb chops. Hold the lamb rack up right with bones sticking straight up with a sharp knife cut straight down between the bones to create even, individual lamb chops. Place the lamb chops in a bowl and pour the second half of the rosemary marinade over the chops, be sure to cover each chop with marinade. Let them stand at room temperature for 20 minutes or refrigerate overnight. Preheat the grill to high heat. When the grill is nice and hot place lamb chops on grill and cook them for about 3–5 minutes on each side for medium-rare.

HAZELNUT CARROT CAKE CUPCAKES WITH HAZELNUT BROWN ALE CREAM CHEESE FROSTING

An easy cake that pairs perfectly with the Rogue Hazelnut Brown Ale. The perfect choice for your beer lover's birthday.

Makes 12 cupcakes

2 cups flour
2 teaspoons baking soda
2 teaspoons baking powder
$1/2$ teaspoon sea salt
$1/2$ teaspoon fresh ground black pepper
2 teaspoons ground cinnamon
1 teaspoon fresh ground nutmeg
1 teaspoon ground ginger
4 whole eggs
$1 1/4$ cups extra virgin olive oil
2 cups sugar
2 teaspoons vanilla
3 cups grated carrots

$1 1/2$ cups chopped hazelnuts
8 ounces cream cheese
4 ounces unsalted butter
$4 1/2$ cups powdered sugar
4 tablespoons Rogue Hazelnut Brown Ale

Preheat oven to 350 degrees. Line 12 portion cupcake pan with cupcake liners. Mix together the first 8 dry ingredients in separate bowl, set aside. Mix together next 4 wet ingredients in large bowl until all are combined. Grate the carrots and chop the hazelnuts. Add the dry ingredients into the wet ingredients a $1/4$ of the bowl at a time, mix until combined, but do not over mix. Stir in the carrots and nuts. Portion the mix into cupcake pan, fill to $3/4$ full per cup. Bake for about 20 minutes. To check insert a toothpick into the center of cupcake; it should come out clean when it's done. The cake will also bounce back when pressed lightly with finger. Cool in the pan for 30 minutes then remove to cool completely.

To make the frosting, combine the cream cheese and butter in a mixer bowl. Mix on medium speed until the butter and cream cheese are soft and fluffy. Slowly add the powdered sugar until it is all incorporated. Add the beer and mix until combined. Decorate cupcakes and serve.

VEGETARIAN DINNER

··

In a big college town like ours, many of our beer-loving customers are vegetarians. They asked that we make sure to add their favorites to the book. So we have included a number of delicious choices, using a variety of fresh, seasonal produce and pairing with some amazing beers. Make the menu whole for your favorite vegetarians, or pick out one or two recipes to add to your favorite meal.

VEGETARIAN BEER DINNER MENU
1st Course
    Chilled Sweet Pea Soup, with mint, crème Fraiche
    Cellar Door Farmhouse Ale, Stillwater Artisanal Ales, Maryland
2nd Course
    Red and Yellow Beet Salad with arugula, herbed goat cheese, Leffe Blonde Vinaigrette
    Leffe Blonde, Abbaye de Leffe S.A, Belgium
3rd Course
    Red Lentils, sautéed edamame, peas, artichoke hearts, asparagus, scallions & grilled radicchio
    Duvel Belgian Strong Pale Ale, Brouwerij Duvel Moortgat NV, Belgium
4th Course
    Apricot Parfait with black pepper mousse and an oatmeal cookie crumble
    Fuller's Vintage Ale, Fuller Smith and Turner PLC, England

FEATURED BEERS

CELLAR DOOR
Made by: Stillwater Artisanal Ales
Style: Farmhouse Ale
From: Maryland
6.6% ABV
Serve in a tumbler

    This beer pours honey, golden color. It has quite a complex flavor profile of grain, yeast, hint of lemon, sage, and a nice spicy finish. Pairs well with mussels, cream, and soft cheese.

LEFFE BLONDE
Made by: Abbaye de Leffe S.A.
Style: Belgian Pale Ale
From: Belgium
6.6% ABV
Serve in a Trappist Glass

    This beer pours crystal clear golden color. It has a balanced flavor of banana, honey, cloves, and a light bready flavor with a slight bitter finish. This beer pairs well with mussels, lobster, salads, creamy cheese.

DUVEL

Made by: Brouwerij Duvel Moortgat NV
Style: Belgian Strong Pale Ale
From: Belgium
8.5% ABV
Serve in a Trappist glass

This beer pours a clear straw color and is very balanced on the taste buds. It tastes of slight spice, citrus, yeast, and some hop bitterness. This beer pairs with seafood and lightly fried foods.

FULLER'S VINTAGE ALE

Made by: Fuller Smith and Turner PLC
Style: Old Ale
From: England
8.5% ABV
Serve in a snifter

This beer pours a slightly hazy copper color with a full bodied, buttery mouthfeel. The prominent flavors are butterscotch, dried fruits, nutty oats, and subtle marzipan. This beer pairs well with desserts, toasted oats, and white chocolate.

RECIPES

CHILLED PEAS SOUP WITH MINT AND CRÈME FRAICHE

This soup is a wonderful light meal starter. It is fresh and cool, combining fresh peas and mint from the garden, then finishing it with a zesty crème.

Serves 6 people

3 cups fresh peas

1 cup heavy cream

$\frac{1}{2}$ cup unsalted butter, melted

12 mint leaves

2 tablespoons farmhouse ale

1 teaspoon sea salt

$\frac{1}{2}$ teaspoon pepper

Cook fresh peas in a medium pot with salted boiling water until tender. Strain the water and shock the vegetables in ice water to stop them from cooking. Heat the heavy cream and butter in a saucepan. Combine the peas, cream, butter, 6 mint leaves, beer, salt, and pepper in a blender. Puree until smooth. Chill and serve with a garnish of crème fraiche and fresh mint.

RED AND YELLOW BEET SALAD WITH ARUGULA, HERBED GOAT CHEESE, AND LEFFE BLONDE VINAIGRETTE

Oh, how we love beets! This is a refreshing beet salad, complimented with crisp arugula and creamy goat cheese. The bright colors and earthy beet flavors sing with a splash of light Leffe vinaigrette.

Serves 6 people

2 large red beets

2 large yellow beets

3 ounces goat cheese, softened

1 teaspoon basil, fine chop

1 teaspoon chives, fine chop

1 teaspoon parsley, fine chop

1 tablespoon olive oil

$1/2$ teaspoon sea salt

$1/4$ teaspoon fresh ground pepper

6 cups arugula

Cook the beets in a large pot of salted, boiling water. Be sure they stay covered completely. Cook until they are tender and a knife goes into them without resistance. Drain the water and place the beets in an ice bath to cool. To peel the beets, gloves are recommended. Under cool running water peel the beets with your hands; the skin should come right off if cooked enough. Cool beets completely and slice into 6 portions. Set aside.

Combine goat cheese, chopped herbs, olive oil, salt, and pepper. Set aside. Dress the arugula with salad dressing and put in the center of your plate. Divide the goat cheese between all your servings and arrange the beets. Serve with your favorite farmhouse saison.

LEFFE BLONDE VINAIGRETTE

This dressing is so light and is full of fresh herbs, it is mild enough to be used with any salad.

Makes $1^1/2$ cups

1 cup extra virgin olive oil

$1/2$ cup Leffe Blond beer

$1/4$ cup honey

1 tablespoon basil, fine chop

1 tablespoon chives, fine chop

1 tablespoon parsley, fine chop

2 cloves garlic, minced

1 teaspoon sea salt

$1/2$ teaspoon fresh ground pepper

Combine all ingredients in a blender except the oil. Blend the ingredients until completely combined and chopped up. Add the oil in a steady stream until all is incorporated. Serve on salad. May be stored for up to 1 week.

RED LENTILS WITH SAUTÉED EDAMAME, PEAS, ARTICHOKE HEARTS, ASPARAGUS, SCALLIONS & GRILLED RADICCHIO

This is a really well balanced dish. We love the different flavors and textures all coming together. These components can all be served separated as side dishes as well.

Serves 6 people

Red Lentils-

$2^1/_2$ cups red lentils

5 cups water

$^1/_2$ teaspoon salt and pepper

$1^1/_4$ teaspoons turmeric

$^1/_2$ cup olive oil

$^1/_2$ teaspoon cumin

3 tablespoons fresh ginger, grated

$^1/_2$ teaspoon hot sauce

$^1/_4$ cup lemon juice

$^1/_4$ cup beer

Vegetable sauté -

6 cups water

4 tablespoons salt

$1^1/_2$ cups edamame

$1^1/_2$ cups peas

12 each asparagus

12-ounce jar prepared artichoke hearts

1 bunch scallions

6 tablespoons olive oil

1 tablespoons blond beer

Salt & pepper to taste

Grilled radicchio-

$1^1/_2$ heads radicchio

6 tablespoons olive oil

Salt and pepper to taste

Cook the lentils first. Wash the lentils and strain them. Place the washed lentils in a medium pot, cover them with water, and bring the lentils to a boil. Stir in the salt, pepper, and the turmeric. Reduce the heat to simmer the lentils for about 25 minutes. Stirring them occasionally, be sure not to over cook them, they should not be mushy.

Heat the olive oil in a sauté pan and add the cumin, hot sauce, and ginger, and sauté for about 1 minute. Add the lentils to the hot sauté pan and mix. Add the lemon juice and beer, sauté for 1 minute more. Set aside in a warm place.

To put the vegetable sauté together you will first blanch the edamame, peas, and asparagus. Bring 6 cups of water and 2 tablespoons of salt to a rolling boil in a medium pot. While the water is heating, set up an ice bath to shock the vegetables immediately after removing them from boiling water. The ice bath should be in a large bowl filled $^2/_3$ full with cold water, ice and the remaining 2 tablespoons salt. Blanch the vegetables one at a time; do not cover the pot while cooking. Begin with the edamame, boil for 4 minutes, and remove with a large slotted spoon into the ice bath. Next you will blanch the peas for 5–6 minutes, remove with a large slotted spoon into the ice bath. Last you will trim the bottoms of the asparagus and blanch for 2–3 minutes, remove and place in the ice bath. It is best to clear the vegetables out of the ice bath before you add the next vegetable. Be sure the water stays cold through this process. This will prevent your vegetables from becoming over cooked, they will stay green and crisp.

Once the vegetables are blanched and cooled, it will be time to sauté them and put your dish together. First you will prepare the radicchio by cutting the radicchio heads in quarters, keeping the center

core in tacked. Drizzle about 1 tablespoon of oil evenly on each quarter of the radicchio, and then sprinkle with salt and pepper. Place the radicchio on a hot grill and cook on each side for about $1^1/_2$ minutes, being careful not to burn it. Set the radicchio aside in a warm place.

Next you will sauté the cold vegetables by adding 6 table-spoons olive oil to a large sauté pan and warming that until it is just at smoking point. Add the arti-choke hearts first and stir to coat them in the oil, then add the eda-mame, peas, asparagus, half the scallions and salt and pepper to taste. Sauté for about 1–2 minutes or until vegetables are hot, be sure to not over cook. Pour the beer into the pan and sauté for 20 more seconds. Remove from the pan.

To set up the final dish you will divide the lentils between the plates, divide the vegetables sauté between the plates and top with a quarter radicchio.

CARAMELIZED APRICOT PARFAIT WITH BLACK PEPPER MOUSSE AND OATMEAL COOKIE CRUMBLES

This really unexpected dessert that combines black pepper and beer into a mousse is both startling and amusing. The Fuller's Vintage ale pairs perfectly with all the elements of this dish.

Serves 6 people

12 fresh apricots
$^1/_2$ cup sugar
1 tablespoon unsalted butter
2 tablespoons vintage ale
12 oatmeal cookies, crumbled (2 cookies per parfait)
3 cups black pepper mousse

Remove the seeds and cut the apricots into small pieces. Combine the sugar and 1 tablespoon of water in a medium sauté pan. Cook the sugar until it becomes a medium caramel color. Add the butter, apricot pieces, and beer. Stir until the apricots are coated, reduce the mix, and cook the apricots for 1 minute. Cool. To assemble the parfait–layer $^1/_3$ of the cookie crumbles on the bottom, then $^1/_4$ cup of mousse, 1 apricot, $^1/_3$ of the cookie crumbles, $^1/_4$ cup mousse, 1 apricot, and finish with $^1/_3$ cookie crumbles. Serve.

OATMEAL COOKIES

When using this cookie recipe for crumbles, cook a little longer for a nice crunch. If serving these beauties by themselves, cook for less time for a nice chewy texture.

Makes 2 dozen

$^1/_2$ cup unsalted butter, softened
$^1/_2$ cup brown sugar
$^1/_3$ cup sugar
2 whole eggs
1 teaspoon vanilla
$^3/_4$ cup all-purpose flour
$^1/_4$ teaspoon baking soda
1 teaspoon cinnamon
$^1/_2$ teaspoon nutmeg
$^1/_2$ teaspoon sea salt
1 $^3/_4$ cups rolled oats
$^1/_2$ cup butterscotch chips

In a mixer with the paddle attachement, combine the butter and sugars. Mix on medium speed until butter is fluffy. Slow the mixer down and add the eggs one at a time, then add vanilla. Mix until all combined. Stop the mixer and add the flour, baking soda, cinnamon, nutmeg, and salt. Mix on slow until just combined. Mix in the oats and then the butterscotch chips. Refrigerate the cookie dough for at least 1 hour or overnight. Preheat the oven to 350 degrees. Drop by rounded spoonfuls on a greased cookie sheet. Bake cookies for about 10–12 minutes for chewy cookies or about 15–18 minutes for cookie crumbles.

WELCOME SPRING

This menu is a veritable toast to the best that spring has to offer. It welcomes the fresh flavors of ramps, asparagus, and watercress. The lightness of perfectly poached quail eggs and tender white sole speak eloquently to spring's rebirth.

Ramps are a once-a-year thing, so we use as much as we can for as long as we can! The beers we chose to pair with this menu are also light, fresh, and complex.

WELCOME SPRING SUPPER MENU

1st Course

Asparagus, poached quail egg, Parmigiano Reggiano, Champagne Beurre Blanc, butter sautéed brioche

Malheur Biere Brut, Brouwerij De Landtsheer NV, Belgium

2nd Course

Butter Poached Dover Sole with ramp pesto, wilted watercress, quinoa risotto

Organic Wiesen Edel-Weiss Hefeweizen, Schneider and Sohn Weissbierbrauerei, Germany

3rd Course

Burnt Pineapple Mousse with crisp almond macaroon, sour cherry compote, praline almond crunch

Sculpin Indian Pale Ale, Ballast Point Brewing Company, California

FEATURED BEERS

MALHEUR BIÈRE DE CHAMPAGNE
Made by: Brouwerij De Landtsheer NV
Style: Bière de champagne
From: Belgium
12% ABV
Serve in a champagne flute

This beer pours cloudy gold with sediment and a frothy white head. The flavor is grassy with lemon, bready malt, a little tart and sharp with a dry finish. This beer pairs well with seafood, toasted bread, hard cheeses, and fresh vegetables.

ORGANIC WIESEN EDEL-WEISS HEFEWEIZEN
Made by: Schneider and Sohn Weissbierbrauerei
Style: Hefeweizen
From: Germany
6.7% ABV
Serve in a Weizen Glass

This beer pours golden with a thick white head. It tastes of hops, bread, yeast, cloves, and balanced malt. This beer pairs well with cured meats, cheese, grains, and sautéed greens.

SCULPIN INDIAN PALE ALE
Made by: Ballast Point Brewing
Style: American IPA
From: California
7% ABV
Serve in a pint glass

This beer pours clear amber color. The flavor is strong grapefruit and citrus with some piney bitterness with a malty finish. This beer pairs well with citrus flavors, pineapple, and salads.

RECIPES

BRIOCHE LOAF

It may be easier to buy this bread in your local bakery, but we find our homemade version irresistible, and we just can't buy those soft, yeasty, buttery smells that fill the house when it is baking.

Makes 1–2 pound loaf
1/4 cup whole milk
1 tablespoon, 1 teaspoon active dry yeast
1 large egg
1³/4 cups unbleached bread flour
1/4 cup sugar
1/4 teaspoon kosher salt
3 large eggs, lightly beaten, room temperature
1¹/4 cups unbleached bread flour
1/3 pound unsalted butter, room temperature

Warm the whole milk to 110 degrees in a small pot. Put the milk, yeast, 1 egg, and 1 cup of flour in the bowl of a heavy duty mixer. Mix the ingredients together with a rubber spatula, mixing just until everything is blended. Sprinkle over the mix with ³/4 cup of flour to cover the yeast mix. Set the yeast mix aside to rest, uncovered for 30–40 minutes.

After this resting time, the flour coating will crack—this is your indication that everything is moving along properly. Add the sugar, salt, 3 eggs, and ³/4 cup of the flour to the yeast mix. Attach the bowl to the mixer with the dough hook. Mix on low speed for a minute or just until the ingredients look as if they are about to come together. On slow but still mixing, sprinkle in the last ¹/2 cup of flour. When the flour is incorporated, increase the mixer speed to medium and beat for about 10 minutes, stopping to scrape down the hook and bowl as needed. The dough will come together, wrap itself around the hook, and slap the sides of the bowl.

When this dough is together, with the mixer on medium-low speed, add the butter a few tablespoons at a time then increase the mixer speed to medium-high speed for a minute, then reduce the speed to medium, and beat the dough for about 5 more minutes, or until the dough is slapping against the sides of the bowl. Be careful to not over work your dough, it should still be cool to the touch when you are finished.

Now transfer the dough to a very large buttered bowl and cover it tightly with plastic wrap. Let the dough rise in a warm spot until it doubles in size, this will take an hour or 2. When the dough has doubled in size, pour it out of the bowl on a lightly floured surface and deflate it by slightly working it back into a loose ball. Return the dough to a buttered bowl. Cover the bowl tightly with plastic wrap and refrigerate the dough for at least 4–6 hours or overnight. The dough will continue to rise, when it is doubled in size again you will pour it out of the bowl on a lightly floured surface and shape into desired shape, place in a oiled pan.

Let the dough rise in a warm spot for about 45 minutes or until it has doubled in the pan. Brush the dough with melted butter and bake in a 375 degree oven for about 30 minutes or until it is golden brown. The bread will sound hollow when the bottom is tapped on. Let bread rest for 30 minutes before slicing.

ASPARAGUS, POACHED QUAIL EGG, PARMIGIANINO REGGIANO, BIERE DE CHAMPAGNE BEURRE BLANC, AND BUTTERED SAUTÉED BRIOCHE

We wait every year for our asparagus plants to sprout, yielding something so special, so tender and so fresh that we are surprised by them every time. Asparagus that has been freshly picked is something to be treasure and celebrated.

Serves 4 people

12 pieces asparagus

2 tablespoons kosher salt

4 quail eggs

3 cups water

3 tablespoons white vinegar

2 pieces brioche, slice $1/2$ inch thick

2 teaspoons salted butter

4 tablespoons Beurre blanc

4 teaspoons shaved Parmigianino Reggiano

Bring a large pot of water to a boil; add the kosher salt and asparagus. Boil uncovered until it reaches al dente about 3–5 minutes. When cooked drain and shock in an ice bath. Set aside.

Bring 3 cups of water and white vinegar to a light simmer in a medium pot. Crack 4 eggs into 4 small dishes, and gently pour the eggs one at a time into the simmering pot of water. Pouring eggs in close to the water will help break the fall and will create eggs that hold together better. Cook eggs for 45 seconds to 1 minute or until the yolks are still soft, but the whites are cooked. Remove gently 1 at a time with a slotted spoon. Set aside in a bowl.

Take the sliced brioche and butter each side with salted butter, sauté in a pan on both sides until golden brown. Slice in half and set half a piece on 4 plates.

Warm asparagus up by returning it to salted boiling water for 45 seconds. Remove from hot water and pat dry. Position the asparagus on the brioche slice, add the poached egg on top of the asparagus, drizzle 1 tablespoon of Beurre blanc on each plate over the egg and shave about 1 teaspoon per plate of cheese over the entire dish. Enjoy!

BIERRE DE CHAMPAGNE BEURRE BLANC

This sauce is a great accompaniment to seafood, vegetables, and lighter meats. It is also very versatile—add fresh herbs and garlic or any beer or wine that complements your dish.

Makes 4–5 tablespoons

1 shallot, peeled and thinly sliced

3 tablespoons butter

3 ounces beer

Sea salt and pepper to taste

In a small sauté pan heat the butter and shallot until shallot becomes translucent. Add the beer and shake and stir the pan until the ingredients become homogenous. Reduce the sauce slightly. The bubbles will begin to slow down when it is the right thickness. Serve warm.

BUTTER POACHED DOVER SOLE

A very light white fish dish, otherwise known as mom's favorite. Poached in butter and paired with ramp pesto and quinoa. The balanced flavors of a hefeweizen round it out beautifully.

Serves 4 people
24 ounces of sole or another light white fish
1 pound of butter
2 tablespoons beer
Sprinkle salt and pepper

We recommend purchasing already cleaned fish filets and sprinkling the filets with salt and pepper. Cut the filets down the middle, roll them up, and skewer them with toothpicks. Melt the butter in a deep, medium saucepan and add the beer. Bring the butter to a light simmer and place 1 portion of fish at a time in the butter; 1 portion should be 6 ounces or 4 rolls at approximately $1\frac{1}{2}$ ounces each. Fish rolls should be submerged in the butter. Simmer for about 2 minutes or until the fish is cooked all the way through. Set aside in a warm place and cook the rest of the fish. Be sure that you do not over fill the butter poach with the fish.

QUINOA RISOTTO

Quinoa is considered a super food and takes on flavor so well. We have made it here "risotto" style by slow cooking while slowly adding a warm liquid.

Makes 3–4 cups

2 cups dry quinoa

4 cups vegetable stock

4 tablespoons unsalted butter

4 tablespoons shallots, thinly sliced

1 teaspoon hefeweizen beer

1 teaspoon salt and pepper

Bring the vegetable stock to a boil. Put the dry quinoa in a separate medium size pan and begin heating over medium heat, stir in $1/2$ a cup of the warm vegetable stock with a wooden spoon, stir until the liquid is absorbed and begins to look dry. Continue adding the warm stock to the quinoa in $1/2$ cup portions and stirring until all absorbed. Continue this process until all the stock is incorporated into the quinoa. The quinoa should be completely cooked.

Season and serve right away or cool down and reheat. To reheat, melt the butter in a sauté pan, cook it until it is lightly browned, add the shallots and beer, sauté for 1 minute then add the quinoa, salt, and pepper. Stir until the quinoa is hot and evenly coated. We prefer the re-heating method because of the great flavor you get from the final shallot-butter sauté.

RAMP PESTO

A marvelous spring time twist on pesto. Ramps have a fresh, green, leek-like flavor which complements basil beautifully. This pesto can be used with fish, chicken, and cheese, and on pasta.

Makes about 1 cup
1 ounce fresh basil leaves
1¹/₂ ounces fresh ramps
1 tablespoon lemon juice
¹/₄ ounce hefeweizen beer
1 ounce pine nuts, toasted
1 ounce parmesan cheese, freshly grated
1 clove garlic, peeled and crushed
¹/₃ cup olive oil
¹/₂ teaspoon salt and freshly ground black pepper

Clean and pick the basil and clean and cut the ramps into medium pieces. Put the basil, ramps, lemon juice, beer, pine nuts, parmesan cheese, garlic, salt, and pepper into a food processor. Blend together until the ingredients are all combined. With the motor still running, pour the oil in a steady stream into the blender until the pesto thickens. Refrigerate for up to 1 week.

WILTED WATERCRESS

Delicate watercress is wonderful sautéed, with a mild flavor that tops even the most tender baby spinach.

Serves 4 people
8 ounces fresh watercress
1 tablespoon oil
1 tablespoon shallot, small dice
Salt and pepper to taste

Place the oil in a large sauté pan, heat over high heat, add the shallot, and cook until translucent. Add the watercress, salt, and pepper. Sauté until the watercress is wilted but not overcooked—this should only take a minute or two. Serve immediately.

BURNT PINEAPPLE MOUSSE

Created to complement the bold flavors of Ballast Point's Sculpin IPA, this mousse has flavors of caramel and tangy pineapple and is balanced with the creamy texture. We have paired this mousse with almond macaroons, sour cherry compote, and praline almonds, but it could be served alone or as a cake filling.

Makes 6 cups

1 pineapple, peeled, cored and cut into medium slices
$1/4$ cup sugar
$1/2$ cup pineapple juice
$1/2$ ounce unflavored gelatin powder
1 cup cold water
6 egg yolks
6 tablespoons sugar
$1^1/2$ cups heavy whipping cream
3 tablespoons IPA beer

Cut the pineapple into medium size slices. In a large, flat bottomed pan add $1/4$ cup of sugar, add a few drops of water to the sugar and mix until it resembles wet sand in texture. Clean the sides of the pan with water and cook over high heat, swirl but do not stir the sugar. Cook until it is a medium caramel color, add the pineapple slices, and cook on one side for 2–3 minutes, until pineapple has a dark caramel color, turn over and cook for another 2–3 minutes.

Add the pineapple juice and cook for 5 minutes. Let cool for 10 minutes and put into a blender. Puree the pineapple until smooth and cool completely. When pineapple is cold begin the rest of the mousse preparation. In a small bowl sprinkle the gelatin powder over 1 cup of ice cold water, mix and let it sit for about 5 minutes. In a mixing bowl add the egg yolks and whisk until they become light yellow and fluffy. While the yolks are being whisked, combine 6 tablespoons sugar and 2 teaspoons of water in a small sauté pan. Cook the sugar until it begins to boil and then cook for 1 minute more. Remove from heat and slowly pour into the egg yolk mix. This is a tricky process, slow the mixer down to slow and pour the hot sugar in a constant but slow stream into the egg yolks, being sure to pour along the inside edge of the bowl, keeping it out of the whisk. When all the sugar is combined with the egg yolks continue to mix until the yolks are cool and hold soft peaks. Place the set-up gelatin in a saucepan and gently melt the gelatin, be sure to warm just until melted, but not overcook. Once the gelatin is melted temper it into the egg yolk mix. Temper the egg-gelatin mix with the pineapple puree, whisk together until smooth. Whisk the heavy cream and IPA beer in a mixing bowl. Whisk until soft peaks form. Gently fold the cream mix into the pineapple mix, do not over mix, as it is important to keep the air in the mix. Refrigerate for at least 4 hours or until set-up. Serve cold.

PRALINE ALMOND CRUNCH

This is a crunchy, sweet almond treat that can be served on its own or as a garnish for desserts.

Makes 1 cup

1 cup slice almonds, lightly toasted
$1/3$ cup sugar
1 teaspoon water
4 teaspoons salted butter
1 teaspoon IPA beer

Lightly toast the almonds, set aside. Combine the sugar and water in a small sauté pan, cook the sugar until it becomes golden brown. Add the butter and IPA to the caramelized sugar, then add the nuts. Stir to coat all the nuts, pour onto a greased cookie sheet. Cool completely and cut into bite size pieces.

SOUR CHERRY COMPOTE

A great accompaniment to desserts, cheese, or ice cream. It can be stored in the refrigerator for up to 2 weeks.

Makes 1 cup

1 cup sour cherries, pitted
4 tablespoons sugar
1 teaspoon lemon juice
1 tablespoon IPA beer

Combine the sugar, lemon juice, and water in a small saucepan, bring to a boil and cook for about 5 minutes. Add the cherries and beer and simmer for another 5 minutes. Cool the compote and serve.

ALMOND MACAROONS

A fancy little cookie that is light and flavorful. This cookie is typically sandwiched with a butter cream filling and can be customized into almost any flavor. We have paired it with our burnt pineapple mousse dessert.

Makes 30 macaroons or 15 filled macaroons

1^1/$_3$ cups almond flour
1^1/$_3$ cups powdered sugar
^{1}/$_2$ cup egg whites
Pinch of cream of tartar
Pinch sea salt
^{1}/$_3$ cup superfine sugar
1 teaspoon vanilla

Preheat the oven on convection at 300 degrees. Combine the almond flour and powdered sugar in a food processor until it is a fine powder. Put the mix through a fine sifter to eliminate any extra lumps. Set aside.

In a mixing bowl add the egg whites, salt, and cream of tartar whisk on medium-high speed until the egg whites double in volume. Reduce the speed and slowly stream the ^{1}/$_3$ cup of sugar into the egg whites, whisk until the egg whites hold a stiff peak and are shiny. Gently fold the almond flour mix into the egg whites, sprinkle ^{1}/$_2$ the almond flour mix over the egg white, and gently fold the mix together. When almond flour is 80 percent incorporated, sprinkle the remaining almond flour on the mix and fold until the flour is completely incorporated and the mix resembles wide ribbons when the spatula is raised. Put the cookie mix into a piping bag with a round tip. We recommend a number 8 tip. Place a piece of parchment paper on a cookie sheet and pipe the batter onto the sheet into about 1 inch circles. Be sure to space the cookies 1 inch apart. Tap the cookie sheet on the counter to remove any peaks on the cookies. Let the cookies rest for 15 minutes. Bake the cookies for about 14–15 minutes. Let them cool completely before removing from the parchment paper. Cookies can be served as is or paired with mousse or ice cream or sandwich cookies together with butter cream, chocolate ganache, or jam.

GRADUATION BRUNCH MENU

Brunch at our pub is a big beer-pairing meal, particularly around graduation and Father's Day. That's why this chapter is a little different than the others. We have decided to present a few of our favorite brunch items to indulge in. These items can be made casually on a Sunday morning at home or made on a larger scale to serve a group. The strata and stuffed French toast are brunch buffet staples, and are always big crowd pleasers.

We serve the Everett Porter with our Steeplechase sandwich, creating a flavor bridge by infusing the French toast bread with this spectacular porter before cooking. It really adds depth of flavor that complements the ham, eggs, cheese, and syrup in this dish.

Another of our favorite pairings is Fuller's London pride with the Full English breakfast. In our minds, there is no better hangover cure. This classic beer has been a favorite of ours for a long time and is a perfect match for a "man's man" breakfast.

GRADUATION BRUNCH MENU

The Full English: 2 Eggs Fried, Peppered Bacon, Irish Banger Sausage, Sautéed Mushrooms, Sautéed Tomatoes, Baked Beans, Toast
London Pride English Pale Ale, Fuller's Smith and Turner, England
Crab Cake Eggs Benedict
River Ale, Deschutes Brewery, Oregon
Steeple Chase French Toast Sandwich
Everett Porter, Hill Farmstead Brewery, Vermont
Caramelized Leek and Havarti Egg Strata
Karnival Kölsch, Stoudts Brewing Company, Pennsylvania
Citrus Cream Cheese Stuffed French Toast
Nelson Imperial IPA, Widmer Brothers Brewing Company, Oregon

FEATURED BEERS

LONDON PRIDE
Made by: Fullers Smith and Turner
Style: English Pale Ale
From: England
4.7% ABV
Serve in English Pint glass

This beer pours a nice golden/amber color. The flavor is lightly bready, caramel malt and a balanced bitter finish. This beer pairs well with fried foods, breads, sandwiches, and sausage.

RIVER ALE
Made by: Deschutes Brewery
Style: American Blonde Ale
From: Oregon
4.0% ABV
Serve in pint glass

This beer pours a hazy golden color with a white foamy head. The flavor is bready and sweet malts, citrus zest, and a spice finish. This beer pairs well with crab, seafood, chicken, eggs, and bread.

EVERETT PORTER
Made by: Hill Farmstead Brewery
Style: American Porter
From: Vermont
7.5% ABV
Serve in pint glass

This beer pours a deep dark brown color with a thick tan head. It tastes of sweet milk chocolate, espresso bitterness, and roasted malt. It pairs well with chocolate, coffee, and bready items.

KARNIVAL KÖLSCH
Made by: Stoudts Brewing Company
Style: Kölsch
From: Pennsylvania
4.8% ABV
Serve in Kölsch glass

    This beer pours a clear golden color with light bready flavor as the backbone, with light citrus, and grassy hops balance to create a clean finish on the palate. Pairs well with cheese, sausage, breads, and fried foods.

NELSON IMPERIAL IPA
Made by: Widmer Brothers Brewing Company
Style: Imperial IPA
From: Oregon
8.6% ABV
Serve in snifter

    This beer pours orange in color with a thick white head. The flavor is loaded with citrusy hops, grapefruit, orange, lemon, and lime. It is very well balanced with a piney aftertaste and a malty backbone. This beer pairs well with cream, citrus flavors, desserts, grilled meats, and spicy foods.

RECIPES

THE FULL ENGLISH BREAKFAST

This is a classic English breakfast. It is hearty, satisfying, and delicious. We have served countless plates of this hangover-curing dish over the years in our restaurant, along with many pints of Fuller's London Pride beer. To take this dish one step further, add black pudding, fried bread, and marmalade.

Serves 2 people
8 ounces button mushrooms
3 tablespoons unsalted butter
4 slices thick cut peppered bacon
4 Irish banger sausage
1 small tomato, cut into 6 pieces
6 ounces English tomato baked beans
4 pieces white toast
4 eggs, over easy
2 tablespoons olive oil
Salt and pepper to taste

Clean and cut the mushrooms into quarters or halves if small and sauté in the butter, salt, and pepper to taste. Sauté until the mushrooms begin to soften, but are not over cooked and mushy. Set aside.

Cook the sausage and bacon in the oven at about 400 degrees until bacon is crisp and sausage is cooked all the way through. Keep warm while assembling the other items. While the sausage and bacon cook, heat the beans in a small pan until they begin to simmer.

Cook the tomato pieces by tossing in a sauté pan with 1 tablespoon olive oil and a pinch of salt and pepper. Slightly sauté for about 1 minute just until the tomato slices are warm and soft, but not falling apart.

Cook the eggs any way you wish: scrambled, fried, or sunny side up. We recommend a nice runny yolk to combine with the other items on the plate. Assemble this dish with 2 pieces of bacon, sausage, 3 tomato slices, half the mushrooms, half the beans, eggs your way, and 2 pieces of toast. Enjoy!

IRISH BANGER SAUSAGE

We began making this traditional sausage at the restaurant because they are not easily available in our area. Making sausage is certainly an art form and we feel this sausage is worth the extra effort. We serve it at breakfast with the full English or with our Bangers and Mash dinner on Tuesday nights.

Makes 20–25, 2¹/₂ ounce sausage links
3¹/₂ pounds pork shoulder, cut into small cubes
1 tablespoons ground black pepper
¹/₂ tablespoon ground ginger powder
¹/₂ tablespoon fresh sage, fine dice
¹/₂ tablespoon mace
3 tablespoons kosher salt
3 ounces bread crumbs, plain
1 cups ice water
Sausage casing

Freeze all of your grinding equipment, as it is very important that your grinder is very cold. Cut the pork shoulder into small pieces, about 1 inch square. Place all the ingredients but the pork shoulder and the water in a food processor. Mix until all the ingredients are a fine crumb. Combine in a large bowl the breadcrumb mix, pork pieces, and the ice cold water. Remove your grinder and set it up, grinding the pork-bread mix through the grinder to a medium grind. Stuff the sausage mix into the casing with a sausage stuffer in about 2¹/₂ ounce links. If you do not have a sausage stuffer but still want to make homemade sausge, simply separate the mix into 2¹/₂ ounce balls and flatten into sausage patties. Refrigerate until ready to cook and serve. When ready to serve, cook the sausage in a hot skillet with a little oil. Sausage takes about 5 minutes to cook.

EGGS BENEDICT

This is a basic recipe for Eggs Benedict of two poached eggs, country ham, and hollandaise on brioche. Use this recipe to build on to make exciting new Benedict flavors. We have included the Crab Cakes Benedict here.

Makes 2 servings
4 poached eggs
6 tablespoons white vinegar
4 pieces country ham
2 piece brioche toasted
6 ounces hollandaise

Bring 6 cups of water and white vinegar to a light simmer in a medium pot. Crack 4 eggs into 4 small dishes and gently pour the eggs one at a time into the simmering pot of water. Pouring eggs in close to the water will help break the fall and will create eggs that hold together better. Cook eggs for 2 minutes or until the yolks are still soft, but the whites are cooked. Remove gently 1 at a time with a slotted spoon. Set aside in a bowl.

Slice the country ham into thin slices and crisp up in a sauté pan. Butter the brioche and grill it in a pan on both sides until it is golden brown and cut each piece in half. Place the two pieces of brioche on a plate, then place the country ham on the brioche, (if making crab cakes eggs Benedict place a crab cake on top of each piece of bread), place the egg on top of the ham (and crab cake), cover the eggs with hollandaise, garnish with tomato diamonds, and thinly sliced chives. Serve immediately.

LUMP CRAB CAKES

Crab Cakes Eggs Benedict pair beautifully with a nice blonde ale. We prefer to serve them with poached eggs, country ham, toasted brioche bread, and spicy remoulade.

Makes 8 3-ounce crab cakes

1 tablespoon olive oil
$1/4$ cup medium white onion, small dice
1 clove garlic, minced
1 small red pepper, small dice
$1/3$ cup fresh parsley, fine dice
1 tablespoon lemon juice
$1/2$ tablespoon Worcestershire sauce
1 egg
$1/8$ cup mayonnaise
$1/2$ tablespoon Dijon
$1/4$ tablespoon Old Bay seasoning
$1 1/2$ cups panko bread crumbs
$1/4$ teaspoon kosher salt
$1/2$ teaspoon pepper
1 pound jumbo lump crab meat
2 tablespoons olive oil

In a large sauté pan heat 1 tablespoon of olive oil and add the onion, garlic, and pepper. Sauté the vegetables for 1 minute and cover. Steam in the covered pan for 4 minutes over medium heat. Remove the cover and sauté for 1 minute longer. Combine the sautéed vegetables, parsley, lemon juice, Worcestershire sauce, egg, mayonnaise, and mustard in a large bowl until combined.

Mix the old bay, bread crumbs, salt, and pepper in a separate bowl until combined. Mix the wet and dry ingredients together. Gently fold the crab into the bread mix, but be sure not to break crab up.

Measure the crab into 3-ounce cakes. In a warm pan add the olive oil and gently place the crab cakes in the pan. Cook on one side until they are lightly browned, flip the crab cakes, and place them in 450 degree oven for about 5 minutes or until firm and golden brown.

EASY HOLLANDAISE SAUCE

This is a variation on the traditional sauce that is easy and reliable. Hollandaise sauce is a perfect accompaniment to breakfast that certainly shouldn't be left in the brunch category. It is also one of our favorite pairings with fresh lobster.

Makes about 1 1/2 cups

2 extra-large egg yolks, room temperature
1 1/4 cups butter
1/8 teaspoon sea salt
1/8 teaspoon fresh ground black pepper
 Pinch cayenne pepper
1 teaspoon lemon juice
1 teaspoon beer (pick the beer that complements your dish)
1 tablespoon water, warm

The first thing to do is clarify your butter by placing the butter in pieces in a small saucepan over very low heat, melting the butter slowly without stirring it. The butter will begin to separate into 3 layers. The top layer is foam, middle layer is the butterfat and the bottom layer is the milk fat and water. With a ladle or large spoon carefully remove the foam layer by gently skimming it off the top of the butterfat layer and discard. Then you will want to separate the butterfat from the water and milk solids. The easiest way to do this is by carefully ladling the yellow butterfat away from the water on the bottom of the pan. You will see the difference in color. Put the butterfat in a separate container and discard the remaining layer.

After the butter is clarified you will want to make sure all of your other ingredients are warm. Place the egg yolks, lemon juice, beer, salt, pepper, and cayenne in a blender and turn on until all the ingredients are combined. Slowly add clarified butter until mixture is thick. Add the water until mixture is smooth then slowly add the rest of the clarified butter. Remove the sauce from the blender and serve immediately.

STEEPLECHASE FRENCH TOAST SANDWICH

A marvelous French toast sandwich with a fried egg, ham, and havarti cheese. It is rich and worth every calorie. We make this with a porter French toast and serve it with the accompanying porter beer.

Makes 2 sandwiches
4 pieces porter French toast
4 ounces sliced ham
4 ounces havarti cheese
2 eggs, over easy

Make the French toast and set aside. Heat the ham in a sauté pan until warm. Fry one egg for each sandwich. Place the ham, eggs, and cheese between two French toast pieces. Serve with a side of maple syrup.

PORTER FRENCH TOAST

Porter makes for a really flavorful, yummy French toast. We prefer to make ours using a thick-cut challah bread, but any thick-cut bread will do. This French toast can be made and served on its own or used for the Steeplechase sandwich in this chapter.

Makes 6 pieces
6 pieces white bread, thick slices
3 whole eggs
1 cup whole milk
4 tablespoons porter beer
1 tablespoon vanilla
$1/8$ teaspoon sea salt
$1/8$ teaspoon fresh ground pepper

Whisk all the ingredients except the bread in a flat bottomed bowl. Slice the challah bread in 1 inch slices, dip the bread in the egg mixture, and cook over medium heat in a large, oiled pan. Cook for about 2 minutes on each side or until golden brown. Serve.

CARAMELIZED LEEK AND HAVARTI EGG STRATA

This is the perfect breakfast meal for a crowd. Assemble it the night before and simply bake it in the morning just before serving. This dish is quite versatile, so be creative with your fillings. It will accommodate sausage, bacon, ham, or any vegetable that speaks to you. This is one of our favorite breakfast dishes; it appears at most of our early morning brunch parties.

Serves 10–12 people

4 leeks, cleaned and thinly sliced

4 tablespoons olive oil

10 whole eggs

2 cups whole milk

$1/2$ cup kölsch beer

2 cloves garlic, minced

2 teaspoons salt and pepper

1 pound white bread, crust removed

6 tablespoons unsalted butter, softened

2 cups Havarti cheese, shredded

Assemble this dish the day before and let it sit overnight, so most of the liquid absorbs into the bread. The first thing to do is clean, slice, and cook the leeks. Leeks can be a pretty dirty vegetable so I recommend rinsing quickly, slicing the leeks, and then washing the slices well in a strainer to get all the dirt out from the layers of the leek. Pat the leeks dry. Place the olive oil in a large, warm pan, add the sliced leeks, and stir them in the pan to coat with some of the oil. Cover the leeks and cook over medium heat for about 3–4 minutes, remove the lid and stir them, cover and cook for another 3–4 minutes. Remove the cover. By now the leeks should be wilted and starting to brown in some spots. Add a sprinkle of salt and pepper to the leeks and stir again. Continue stirring the leeks until the pieces are tender and the whole dish begins to turn a light golden brown color. Remove from the pan and set aside to cool.

Next you will mix your eggs, milk, beer, garlic, 1 teaspoon salt, and pepper in a medium bowl, whisk ingredients until all combined.

To assemble the strata, cut the crust off the bread and butter one side of each slice, line the bottom of a 9"x13" inch baking dish with some of the bread slices, butter side down. Spread half the caramelized leeks on the first layer of bread and then spread a third of the shredded cheese over the leeks. Layer another layer of buttered, crustless bread on top of the cheese layer. Next spread the remainder of the leeks on the layer of bread, sprinkle with a third of the cheese, layer the last layer of buttered, crustless bread on top of the cheese. Sprinkle evenly the remaining cheese on the very top of the strata, next you will pour the egg mixture over the whole dish, and wrap the baking dish tightly all the way around the dish. Use a plate or another baking dish to weigh the bread down. Store overnight in the refrigerator. When ready to serve, preheat the oven to 350 degrees and bake for about 1 hour. The strata will be puffy and golden brown when finished. Serve hot.

CITRUS CREAM CHEESE STUFFED FRENCH TOAST

This is a delightful and easy dish to prepare for a larger group. The sweet cream cheese sandwiched between thick slices of bread is baked all together in a spiced egg mix. Make this the day before and bake before serving.

Serves 10–12 people

1 pound cream cheese, softened
$^1/_2$ cup orange juice
$^1/_4$ cup imperial IPA beer
Zest of 1 orange, 1 grapefruit, and 1 lime
1$^1/_4$ cups sugar
12 whole eggs
2 cups whole milk
2 cups half and half
1 tablespoon vanilla
1 teaspoon nutmeg
$^1/_2$ teaspoon sea salt
1$^1/_2$ pounds white bread, thick slices
6 tablespoons butter

In a mixer with the paddle attachment, add the cream cheese and beat in the mixer until softened and a little fluffy. Add the citrus zest, $^1/_2$ cup of sugar, beer, and orange juice, mixing, until all combined. Add 2 eggs and mix until all combined, set aside.

Combine the 10 eggs, milk, half and half, vanilla, $^1/_2$ cup of sugar, nutmeg, and salt, whisk in a medium bowl. Slice the bread in thick slices and remove the crust. We prefer challah or brioche bread for this recipe, but any thick white bread will do. Butter half the slices of bread on one side.

In a 13"x9" baking dish line the first layer of bread, butter side down in the bottom of the pan. Spread the cream cheese mix evenly over the layer of bread, and layer the rest of the bread on top of the cream cheese filling. Pour the egg mix over the entire dish, wrap the baking dish tightly all the way around the dish. Use a plate or another baking dish to weigh the bread down. Store overnight in the refrigerator. When ready to serve, preheat the oven to 350 degrees and bake for about 1 hour, the French toast will be puffy and golden brown when finished. Serve hot with syrup.

SUMMER

In summer the days are long and hot. An ice cold Kölsch is a welcoming refreshment. Our menus in this section celebrate the fun that summer brings. Outdoor parties celebrating barbeque in the south and lobster in the North. We embrace the sand and surf, the warm breeze on the beach paired with fresh sorbet and lambic. We focus on vegetables straight from the garden and lighter witbier and pilsners.

SUMMER BIRTHDAY BASH

A steamy summer evening on the patio, fireflies twinkling, and a birthday to celebrate—what could be better? These dishes come straight out of the garden. A pop of fresh herbs, cool cucumber, and watermelon start the meal off with bright notes that pair beautifully with the Allagash White. The centerpiece is a perfectly roasted chicken surrounded by vegetables fresh from the garden or farmer's market. Wrap up with a fun twist on Grandma's strawberry rhubarb pie. This version is light, airy, and full of flavor. We designed this pie specifically for the Liefman's Fruitesse beer—you will never look at rhubarb the same way again.

SUMMER BIRTHDAY BASH MENU

1st Course

    Watermelon Salad with watermelon, cucumber, feta cheese, mint, and basil

    Cool Cucumber Vinaigrette

    Allagash White, Allagash Brewery, Maine

2nd Course

    Roasted Chicken with tomatoes, eggplant, summer squash, and fresh herbs

    Reissdorf Kölsch, Brauerei Heinrich Reissdorf, Germany

3rd Course

    Strawberry Rhubarb Icebox Pie

    Liefmans Fruitesse, Brouwerij Liefmans, Belgium

FEATURED BEERS

ALLAGASH WHITE

Made by: Allagash Brewing Company

Style: witbier

From: Maine

5% ABV

Serve in weizen glass

This beer pours cloudy yellow with a nice white head. This is a great example of a witbier. It is refreshing with hints of citrus, grain, and light spice notes. This beer pairs well with herbs, salads, sushi, and salty cheese.

REISSDORF KÖLSCH

Made by: Brauerei Heinrich Reissdorf

Style: Kölsch

From: Germany

4.8% ABV

Serve in Kölsch glass

This beer pours a clear golden color with lightly toasted grains, crackers, and biscuits as a flavor backbone, and herbal-grassy hops balance to create a clean finish on the palate. Pairs well with cheese, sausage, breads, and fried foods.

LIEFMANS FRUITESSE

Made by: Brouwerij Liefmans

Style: Fruit beer

From: Belgium

4.2% ABV

Serve in flute or tumbler with ice

This beer pours cherry red and is pleasantly sparkling and refreshing. The flavors are cherry, strawberry, and sour rhubarb. This beer is a perfect aperitif or pairing with tart desserts.

RECIPES

WATERMELON SALAD

A big favorite when the weather turns hot. We have put watermelon alongside cucumber, feta cheese, mint, basil, and a light cool cucumber vinaigrette.

Serves 6 people
$1/2$ large watermelon, cut or balled into bite size pieces
1–2 cucumbers, cut or balled into bit size pieces
6 ounces feta cheese
12 leaves basil, chiffonade
12 leaves mint, chiffonade
3–4 ounces vinaigrette

Clean and cut the watermelon and cucumber, and combine these ingredients in a salad bowl. Cut or crumble the feta cheese up into bite size pieces into the salad bowl, and add the chiffonade basil and mint. Feel free to tear the herbs into small pieces if you prefer. Sprinkle the vinaigrette over the salad right before serving, gently toss the ingredients together, being sure not to over mix. Serve cold.

COOL CUCUMBER VINAIGRETTE

A crisp, refreshing vinaigrette. We have made it with Allagash White beer, but any witbier will do. This dressing will complement any fresh salad.

Makes $1^1/2$ cups
1 cucumber, peeled, seeded and sliced
$1/4$ cup extra virgin olive oil
2 tablespoons witbier
2 tablespoons yogurt
1 tablespoon agave syrup
4 tablespoons mint, finely chopped
1 teaspoon sea salt
$1/2$ teaspoon fresh ground pepper

Combine all ingredients in a blender except the oil. Blend the ingredients until completely combined and chopped up. Add the oil in a steady stream until all incorporated. Serve on salad. May be stored for up to 3 days.

ROASTED CHICKEN WITH SAUTÉED SUMMER VEGETABLES

A perfectly roasted chicken is hard to beat. This one is paired with fresh vegetables from the garden in the heart of summer. We grow a variety of heirloom tomatoes, fresh summer squash, fresh herbs, and eggplant, but the farmer's market will yield the best of all these ingredients.

Serves 4 people

1 whole chicken
2 tablespoons unsalted butter
3 tablespoons olive oil
1 shallot, thinly sliced
1 clove garlic, minced
1 eggplant, medium dice
12 sprigs fresh parsley, leaves picked
1 tablespoon fresh rosemary, finely chopped
1 tablespoon fresh thyme, finely chopped
2 yellow squash, medium dice
2 zucchini, medium dice
2 medium heirloom tomatoes, medium dice
2 tablespoons Kölsch beer
Sea salt and pepper to taste

Preheat your oven to 500 degrees. Place the chicken in a baking pan and rub the butter all over the outside and inside. Sprinkle with salt and pepper. When oven is 500 degrees, put the chicken uncovered in the oven. Cook it for about 15–20 minutes to create a nice sear on the outside. The skin should be golden brown in color. When the outside is nice and golden brown, turn the oven down to 425 degrees and bake for about 1 hour. Remove the chicken and let it rest while you prepare the vegetables.

In a large sauté pan heat the olive oil over high heat. Add the shallot and garlic, sauté until shallot becomes translucent. Add the eggplant and sauté for 30 seconds, then add the fresh herbs and sauté 30 more seconds. Add the zucchini and squash, sauté about 1 minute. Add the tomatoes, beer, salt, and pepper. Sauté for 1–2 minutes. Be sure not to overcook the vegetables; you want them to be juicy and soft, but not mushy. Serve immediately with your freshly roasted chicken and a nice cold Kölsch beer.

STRAWBERRY RHUBARB ICEBOX PIE

This is a unique pie, and an adult twist on the strawberry rhubarb pies of childhood. The sour rhubarb complements the sweet strawberries perfectly, but the cream cheese and the fruitesse beer take it over the top.

Makes 2 9-inch pies
2 cups graham cracker crumbs
2 tablespoons unsalted butter, melted
$^1/_2$ cup sugar

Pinch sea salt
1 quart strawberries, cleaned and cut in half
1 rhubarb stalks, cleaned and cut into $^1/_2$ inch pieces
$1^1/_2$ cups sugar
4 tablespoons fruit beer
4 egg yolks
$^1/_4$ ounce gelatin
$^1/_2$ cup ice cold water
8 ounces cream cheese
1 cup heavy whipping cream

Preheat oven to 350 degrees. Combine the graham cracker crumbs, butter, sugar, and salt in a bowl. Pour this mix into a buttered pie dish and press the mix evenly around the dish, up the sides and on the bottom. Bake for 10 minutes in the oven. Remove and let cool completely.

To make the pie filling, start by cleaning and cutting the strawberries and rhubarb. Combine the strawberries, rhubarb, one cup of sugar, and fruit beer in a large pot. Cook over medium-high heat for about 15 minutes or until the rhubarb has completely lost its shape. When the fruit has cooked down and becomes slightly liquidy, remove from the heat and let cool for 10 minutes. Then pour the strawberry mix into a blender, puree this mix together until it is completely smooth. Remove from blender and cool completely.

When the strawberry mix is cold begin preparing the remaining ingredients. Combine the gelatin powder with $^1/_2$ cup cold water, let it sit for about 5 minutes. In a mixing bowl add the egg yolks and whisk until they become light yellow and fluffy. While the yolks are being whisked, combine $^1/_2$ cup of sugar and $^1/_2$ teaspoon water in a small sauté pan. Cook the sugar until it begins to boil and then cook for 1 minute more, remove from heat and slowly pour into the egg yolk mix. (This can be a tricky process, slow the mixer down to low and pour the hot sugar in a constant but slow stream into the egg yolks, being sure to pour along the inside edge of the bowl, keeping it out of the whisk).

When all the sugar is combined with the egg yolks continue to mix until the yolks are cool and hold soft peaks. Remove the egg yolks from the mixing bowl and put into a medium size bowl, set aside. In the mixing bowl add the cream cheese and beat with the paddle attachment until fluffy and light. Gently fold the egg yolks and the cream cheese together. Place the gelatin in a saucepan and gently melt the gelatin and temper the gelatin into the egg yolk mix. Temper the egg-gelatin mix with the cold, strawberry puree, whisk together until smooth. Whisk $^1/_2$ cup whipping cream in a mixing bowl. Whisk until soft peaks form. Gently fold the cream mix into the strawberry mix. Do not over mix, as it is important to keep the air in the mix. Refrigerate for at least 4 hours or until set-up. Serve cold.

LOBSTER BAKE

I grew up in Maine so this chapter is very dear to my heart. The sweet salty smell of the ocean breeze, the orange and red sunsets filling the sky and reflecting off the ocean, and the sound of the waves hitting the rocky coast. When I think of Maine, I think of old friends and close family, I see lobster boats floating on the rough sea and barnacle-covered buoys scattered on lawns, floating in the harbor and hanging from eves of garages.

We have been lucky enough to have shared some of this lifetime with a dear friend. Although he has passed, we will always cherish the memories of Dick Ames, and how he touched our hearts, our minds, and our bellies. Dick was quite the cook and lobsterman, along with being our favorite attorney, and we dedicate this chapter to him and his lovely wife Patty Ames. We have included Dick's famous stuffed clams recipe in this chapter and have paired it with a remarkable local beer right out of Portland, Maine—Allagash Dubbel Reserve. The rest of the menu is simple and straightforward in order to underscore the delicacy of lobster and clams straight from the sea.

To finish this messy, yet delectable meal, we have included a family staple, Blueberry Beer Cake—creamy and packed with wild Maine berries. Cheers to old friends and full bellies!

LOBSTER BAKE MENU

DICK'S STUFFED CLAMS
Allagash Dubbel Reserve, Allagash Brewery, Maine

STEAMED CLAMS WITH CLARIFIED BUTTER
Red Claws Ale, Gritty McDuff's Brewery, Maine

STEAMED LOBSTER WITH CORN ON THE COB AND CREAMY POTATO SALAD
Shipyard Summer Ale, Shipyard Brewing, Maine

BLUEBERRY BEER CAKE
Bar Harbor Blueberry Ale, Atlantic Brewing Company, Maine

FEATURED BEERS

ALLAGASH DUBBEL RESERVE
Made by: Allagash Brewing Company
Style: Belgian style dubbel
From: Maine
7% ABV
Serve in Trappist glass

This beer pours deep red in color. This is a complex malty beer, with Belgian fruitiness, a hint of chocolate, and nuts. This beer pairs well with beef stew, hearty clam and mussel dishes, cheeses, and chocolate desserts.

RED CLAWS ALE
Made by: Gritty McDuff's Brewery
Style: Irish Red Ale
From: Maine
Serve in Pint glass

This beer pours a dark red amber color with malty, nutty, and roasted flavors finishing with floral hops. This beer is a easy drinking session beer. Pairs well with fried foods, butter, cream soups, and sandwiches.

SHIPYARD SUMMER ALE
Made by: Shipyard Brewing
Style: American Pale Wheat Ale
From: Maine
4.8% ABV
Serve in Pint glass

This beer pours a cloudy light golden color. This easy-to-drink beer has a mellow malted wheat flavors and is not overly hopped. This beer pairs well with seafood.

BAR HARBOR BLUEBERRY ALE
Made by: Atlantic Brewing Company
Style: Fruit beer
From: Maine
Serve in Pint glass

This beer pours a coppery brown. This is a light fruit ale made with wild Maine blueberries. The taste has sweet fruit up front with bready elements and a slightly bitter finish. This beer pairs well with salads and dessert.

RECIPES

DICK'S STUFFED CLAMS

These clams always remind me of the coast of Maine and our dear friend Dick. They are stuffed full of flavor and pair beautifully with nice brown ale. We make big batches and freeze them so we can pull out a few for appetizers anytime.

Makes 35 to 40 stuffed clams

20 quahog clams, at least 3 inches in diameter
12 ounces Italian sausage, removed from casings and crumbled
8 ounces chorizo sausage, any casings removed
8 tablespoons unsalted butter
1 cup yellow onion, finely diced
$1/2$ cup red bell pepper, finely diced
$1/2$ cup celery, finely diced
3 cups bread crumbs
$1/2$ cup beer

Preheat the oven to 350 degrees.

Rinse clams several times until free of any sand and dirt. Put the clams in a large saucepan and add cold water to a depth of two inches. Cover the pan tightly and steam over high heat for 4 to 5 minutes, or until the clams open. Drain the clams and discard any that do not open. Let the clams cool slightly, and then remove the meat from the shells. Reserve the clamshells. Chop the clams finely in a food processor and set aside.

In a large sauté pan, brown the Italian sausage over medium heat, breaking up with a wooden spoon into small chunks, about 10 minutes. Add the chorizo to the skillet and cook, stirring, for another 5 minutes or until all meat is cooked. Scrape the sausage into a bowl, leaving the drippings in the pan.

Add the butter to the skillet and melt over medium-high heat. Add the onion, pepper, celery, and cook, stirring, for about 5 minutes, or until the vegetables soften. Add the 3 cups of breadcrumbs, the chopped clams, the cooked sausage, and $1/2$ cup of beer. Mix well, adding more breadcrumbs or liquid as necessary to make a mixture that holds together when squeezed.

Lightly pack the clamshells with stuffing and place on baking sheets. Cover the baking sheets with foil and bake for 20 minutes. Remove the foil and continue to bake until the stuffing is lightly browned, 10 to 20 more minutes.

STEAMED LOBSTER AND STEAMED CLAMS

There are a lot of ways to prepare lobster and clams. We have made these two wonderful ingredients into soups, bread pudding, pastas and casseroles, but we have always come back to the basics—a steamed lobster with clams. This really is the best way to enjoy them, dipped in butter and paired with a light summer beer.

Serves 4 people

2 pounds clams
1 cup kosher salt
2 gallons cold water
4 2-pound lobsters
3 quarts water
2 cups wheat beer
3 teaspoons kosher salt
2 teaspoons peppercorns
4 celery stalks, medium dice
1 medium white onion, medium dice
2 bay leaves
1 pound salted butter, melted

Clean clams well. For best results, prepare a brine of $1/2$ cup of salt and 1 gallon of cold water. Soak the clams in the brine for 15 minutes. Drain the brine and make a fresh one of $1/2$ cup of salt and 1 gallon of cold water, soaking the clams for another 15 minutes in this brine. This process really cleans the clams out so you can avoid eating sand and enjoy the creamy texture of the clam meat. After the second brine, remove the clams and scrub the shells clean under cold running water. Set aside.

Use the same steaming liquid and pot for the lobster and clams. You will need a large stock pot and a steamer basket. Combine 3 quarts of water, the beer, 3 teaspoons salt, peppercorns, the celery, onion, and bay leaves. Bring this mix to a rolling boil. Insert the steam basket and lobsters. Cook the lobsters for about 15 minutes. The lobster will turn bright red and the legs will easily pull off when ready.

If you are cooking clams as well, keep the water boiling and place the clams in the steam basket. Clams will take about 5–10 minutes to cook, they are finished cooking when they open up. Discard any shells that do not open. Serve immediately.

CREAMY POTATO SALAD

This is a lovely, light potato salad. Serve this at any barbeque, lobster bake, or cookout.

Serves 8 people
2 pounds red bliss potatoes
1 teaspoons salt
$^1/_2$ cup Dijon vinaigrette
1 cup mayonnaise
$^1/_2$ cup sour cream
1 teaspoon lemon zest
1 teaspoon sea salt
1 teaspoon pepper
4 whole eggs, hardboiled and cut in small dice
1 cup celery, small dice
1 cup carrots, small dice
$^1/_4$ cup chives, small dice

Place the potatoes in a large pot and cover them with water. Add one teaspoon salt and bring the potatoes to a boil, reduce to medium heat, and cover. Cook the potatoes for about 15–20 minutes or until a fork inserts without resistance. When the potatoes are cooked, drain them and cool completely. Cut the potatoes into bite-sized pieces.

In a separate bowl, combine the vinaigrette, mayonnaise, sour cream, lemon zest, salt, and pepper, whisk these ingredients together. In a large bowl combine the potato pieces, hardboiled eggs, celery, carrots, and chives, pour the mayonnaise mix over the vegetables and gently mix until all the potatoes are covered.

DIJON VINAIGRETTE

This is a versatile vinaigrette and can be used on any salad, in potato salad, in pasta salad, or as a marinade. We have picked wheat beer to go into this dressing, but almost any light beer would work well.

Makes about 2$^1/_2$ cups
1 $^1/_2$ cups extra virgin olive oil
$^3/_4$ cup wheat beer
$^1/_3$ cup Dijon mustard
Pinch of salt and pepper

Combine all ingredients in a blender except the oil. Blend the ingredients until completely combined. Add the oil in a steady stream until all incorporated. Serve on salad. May be stored for up to 1 week.

BLUEBERRY BEER CAKE

We love to make blueberry beer by crushing a few into the bottom of a glass and then adding a light ale. This cake pairs beautifully and the splash of blueberry beer in the custard creates a nice bridge.

Serves 10 people

1^1/$_2$ cups all-purpose flour
^{1}/$_2$ cup sugar
^{1}/$_2$ cup butter, softened
1^1/$_2$ teaspoons baking powder
1 large egg
1^1/$_2$ teaspoon vanilla
1 quart fresh blueberries
3 cups whole sour cream
3 large egg yolks
^{3}/$_4$ cup sugar
2 tablespoons blueberry beer

Preheat oven to 350 degrees and grease 9" spring form pan.

Combine the first 6 ingredients in mixer, and mix until it forms a ball. Spread this mix evenly on the bottom of the spring form pan and set aside. In a separate bowl combine the sour cream, egg yolks, sugar, and beer. Evenly distribute the blueberries on top of the dough in the spring form pan and pour the sour cream mix over the blueberries in the pan. Bake for about 1 hour or until edges are lightly browned and middle is lightly giggly. Refrigerate for at least 3 hours. This cake must be completely cool before removing from the pan to prevent it from falling apart.

PARTY AT THE BEACH

Every year we have the great pleasure of visiting with family on the coast of North Carolina. We look forward to relaxing from our hectic schedule, spending time with loved ones and feeling the sweet, salty breeze blowing in our hair. But Luther can never quite separate himself from his passion for food and great beer. We always go seafood crazy by the ocean, and try to enjoy the fresh, sweet fish and seafood every chance we get.

The seafood tower is the perfect start to a summer eve next to the ocean, sitting in our Nags Head hammock chairs and watching the sunset. We have paired it with the DeuS Biere de Champagne because of the light, delicate, champagne-like flavor that enhances the fresh seafood. You do not have to be at the beach to enjoy these dishes and beers; they really shine anywhere you are.

PARTY AT THE BEACH MENU
1st Course
    Cold Seafood Tower of lobster, crab, shrimp, oysters, mussels and clams.
    DeuS Brut des Flandres, Brouwerij Bosteels, Belgium
2nd Course
    Slow Roasted Ribeye with tempura battered soft shell crab, grilled asparagus, and hollandaise
    Pliny the Elder, Russian River Brewing Company, California
3rd Course
    Strawberry Sorbet
    Organic Strawberry Fruit Ale, Samuel Smith's Old Brewery, England

FEATURED BEERS

DEUS BRUT DES FLANDRES
Made by: Brouwerij Bosteels
Style: Biere de Champagne
From: Belgium
11.5% ABV
Serve in flute

    This beer pours light and clear, resembles champagne in color and effervescence. This beer tastes of light fruits pear, apples, and light citrus. It has hints of spicy esters, white pepper, and cloves. This beer is smooth and mellow. This beer pairs with seafood, fresh fruits, and vegetables.

PLINY THE ELDER
Made by: Russian River Brewing Company
Style: Imperial IPA
From: California
Serve in Pint glass

    This beer pours clear orange with a white head. This beer has bitter hops upfront, transitions into sweet malt, grapefruit and a slight fruitiness. This beer pairs well with red meats, barbeque, cheese, and citrus-flavored desserts.

ORGANIC STRAWBERRY FRUIT ALE
Made by: Samuel Smith's Old Brewery
Style: fruit beer
From: England
5.2% ABV
Serve in flute

    This beer pours a hazy red color and tastes like sweet strawberries with some creaminess and a touch of bitter hops. This beer pairs with strawberry desserts, salads, cheese.

RECIPES

COLD SEAFOOD TOWER

An impressive display of seafood, as delicious as it is beautiful. This dish is perfect for parties or a dinner for two. We have combined lobster, crab, shrimp, clams, mussels, and oysters, but feel free to choose your favorite seafood items.

Serves 4 people

2 live lobsters
4 snow crabs
1 pound of shrimp
1 pound clams
$^1/_2$ pound mussels
$2^1/_2$ gallons water
$^1/_4$ cup kosher salt
2 cups beer
2 teaspoons lemon juice
12 sprigs parsley
1 tablespoon peppercorns
1 tablespoon thyme
3 carrots, peeled and medium dice
3 celery stalks, medium dice
1 medium white onion, medium dice
12 fresh oysters, shucked on half shell
1 lemon, cut in wedges
1 lime, cut in wedges

Combine in a 3 quart stock pot: $2^1/_2$ gallons of water, the beer, salt, peppercorn, lemon juice, parsley, thyme, carrots, celery, and onion. Bring the stock pot to a boil and for about 5 minutes. Add the lobsters to the pot and cook for about 10 minutes or until the lobster is bright red. Remove the lobster from the water and place in an ice bath. Allow the water to return to a full boil. Add the crab to the boiling water and cook for about 7 minutes or until the crab is bright red. Remove from the crab and place in the ice bath.

Let the water come back to a boil and add the shrimp, cooking the shrimp for about 6 minutes. Remove from the water and put in the ice bath. Return to a boil and add the clams and mussels. Cook for about 4–5 minutes or until the shells open. Remove the mussels and clams from the water and ice down. Throw out any shells that do not open. Refrigerate the seafood for several hours to be sure it is cold. When you are ready to serve the seafood, arrange on a three-tiered tower and add the shucked oysters, lemon, and lime wedges. Serve with spicy remoulade, cocktail sauce, or mignonette.

TEMPURA BATTERED SOFT SHELL CRABS

This tempura batter can be used for almost anything. We use it for onion rings, fried shrimp, and tempura vegetables. It makes a nice crunchy, light batter.

Makes 4 crabs
$1/2$ cup Hefe-Weizen beer
$1/2$ cup cold water
1 large egg yolk
2 tablespoons sesame oil
$1/3$ cup all-purpose flour
$1/8$ cup cornstarch
4 soft shell crabs
8 cups vegetable oil

Preheat fryer to 350 degrees. If you do not have a fryer, you can create a deep fryer with a large stockpot. Pour the oil into the pot and heat to 350 degrees.

Mix the dry ingredients in a medium bowl and set aside. Mix the wet ingredients in a medium bowl and set aside. Keep all wet ingredients in an ice bath with kosher salt at all times. It is essential that all the ingredients stay ice cold or else the batter will not puff up and crunch properly.

Dip the crab into the batter and let the excess drip off. Carefully place the battered crabs into the hot oil one at a time. Fry until the crabs begin to float and the batter is golden brown, about 3–5 minutes.

Remove from fryer onto a paper towel-lined plate. Serve immediately.

SLOW ROASTED RIBEYE

This is a nice and easy way to prepare a juicy steak: marinated and then roasted in the oven.

Serves 4 people
2 pounds boneless ribeye
1 cup olive oil
1 cup IPA beer
$1/2$ cup dry mustard
1 teaspoon kosher salt
1 teaspoon pepper

Combine the beer, dry mustard, salt, and pepper in a blender until all combined. With the blender on medium speed, stream the oil into the blender until the marinade is homogenous. Rub the marinate all over the ribeye, wrap with plastic and marinate for a minimum of 2 hours and a maximum of 2 days.

When ready to cook, remove the plastic wrap and wrap the meat in aluminum foil. Bake the ribeye in a 325 degree oven for about 30–40 minutes or until it reaches the desired temperature. We recommend medium-rare which will measure at 135 degrees. Let your ribeye rest for about 10 minutes before slicing.

GRILLED ASPARAGUS

Sweet and simple, with just a touch of fire to bring out their flavor.

2 bunches fresh asparagus
2 tablespoons olive oil
Salt and pepper, to taste

Trim the bottom ends off asparagus, cut the bottom ½ inch off where asparagus is dry and not as tender. Coat the asparagus with oil, salt, and pepper.

Roast in 425 oven for 5 minutes, or grill for 3–5 minutes or until tender. Serve immediately.

STRAWBERRY SORBET

Nothing beats a homemade sorbet, especially with in-season fruit. This one is light, refreshing, sweet and a little tart.

Makes 1 quart

$^3/_4$ cup sugar

$^1/_4$ cup strawberry beer

$1^1/_2$ pounds fresh strawberries, cleaned

1 tablespoon lemon juice

$^1/_4$ teaspoon sea salt

In a small saucepan, combine the sugar and beer. Cook until the sugar is completely dissolved. Cool the sugar mix completely. In a blender combine the strawberries, beer syrup, lemon juice, and salt. Blend until the mix is a smooth puree. Refrigerate the puree for 4–6 hours or until completely chilled. Churn the sorbet mix in an ice cream maker according to the manufacturer's directions. This sorbet will last in the freezer for up to one month.

SMOKIN' BARBEQUE MENU

A sunny afternoon, good music, and better food. Yes, that's all we need, especially when the band is our favorite Charlottesville trio. Our barbecues are always buffet style. That way, people can come and go, grazing as they please. Recreate this menu in its entirety or just choose the recipes that speak to you.

We have paired this food with a variety of beers from smoked beer, a super hoppy IPA to an even stronger ale. But the beauty of barbecue is that it loves beer, so make your own picks. Just remember to enjoy your juicy, falling off the bone smoked pork and ribs smothered in our very own Gartrell's Epic Beer Barbeque sauce.

SMOKIN' BARBECUE MENU

Stationed Buffet

Station 1:

    Smoked Pork Belly, with creamy corn grits, tomato jam, onion pork jus

    The original Schlenkerla Rauchbier Märzen, Heller-Bräu Trum GmbH, Germany

Station 2:

    Ribs and Rings

    Terrapin Hopsecutioner, Terrapin Beer Company, Georgia

Station 3:

    Collard Greens with country ham and brown sugar

    Sweet Onion Hush Puppies

    Roasted Okra

    Piraat Ale, Brouwerij Van Steenberge N.V., Belgium

Station 4:

    Peach Crisp with whipped cream

    Lindemans Pêche, Brouwerij Lindemans, Belgium

FEATURED BEERS

THE ORIGINAL SCHLENKERLA RAUCHBIER MÄRZEN
Made by: HellerBräu Trum GmbH
Style: Smoked beer
From: Germany
5.1% ABV
Serve in a dimple mug

This bottom fermented smoked beer pours a dark, hazy brown color. The smoked flavor is balanced with a hint of sweetness and a touch of grain. This beer pairs well with smoked meats.

HOPSECUTIONER
Made by: Terrapin Beer Company
Style: American IPA
From: Georgia
7.3% ABV
Serve in a pint glass

This beer pours a nice golden color with a thick white head. This beer is hops and more hops. The flavors profile is citrus, caramel malt with a bitter finish. Pair this beer with fried foods, smoked meats, and barbeque sauce.

PIRAAT ALE

Made by: Brouwerij Van Steenberge N.V.
Style: Belgian Strong Ale
From: Belgium
10.5% ABV
Serve in a beer Trappist glass or tulip glass

This beer pours a clear golden color with a thick white head. The flavor is fruity apple with citrus zest. It has a spicy, floral flavor with a balanced malt finish. It pairs well with roasted vegetables, smoked meats, fried foods, and fruit desserts.

LINDEMANS PÊCHE

Made by: Brouwerij Lindemans
Style: Lambic
From: Belgium
2.5% ABV
Serve in a stem glass

This beer pours a golden color with a white head. The flavor is predominately sweet, fresh peaches with some fruity malt and light oak. This beer pairs well with peaches and fruity desserts, cheese, salad, and waffles.

RECIPES

SMOKED PORK BELLY WITH ONION PORK JUS

You want to talk about creamy, fatty, smoked goodness? Well here it is. This dish is not for the faint of heart—it is rich and fatty and downright decadent. We have paired it with our creamy corn grits and tomato jam which really takes this dish to another level. Drink it with a glass of The Original Schlenkerla Rauchbier.

Serves 4-6 people
2^1/$_2$ pounds pork belly
1 gallon and ^{1}/$_2$ cup smoked beer
2 cups Gartrell's Dry Rub
1 cup white onion, small dice

Marinate the pork belly in one gallon of beer for 24 hours in the refrigerator. (This step is optional, but absolutely worth the extra effort. The beer will not only infuse extra flavor into the meat, but will also help tenderize it).

After the pork has marinated, remove it from the beer and discard the beer used for marinating. Rub it with 2 cups of Gartrell's Dry rub. Place it in a smoker at 180 degrees; place a large oven safe pan underneath the pork belly to catch all of the drippings. Cook the belly for 12–14 hours or until it is tender and easily pulls apart. We prefer to smoke with oak wood, but other smoking woods that

we recommend are hickory, apple wood, and mesquite. When the pork belly is done, set it aside and finish the jus. Pour the pork drippings that were collected from smoking in a saucepan with the diced onion. Simmer the liquid until the onions are soft. Turn the jus off and skim the top layer of fat. Add the ^{1}/$_2$ cup fresh smoked beer to your sauce and serve with sliced pork belly.

CREAMY CORN GRITS

Move over instant grits, these slow cooked grits are moving in and you will never go back to that easy and fast version. If you want to impress your friends and family with your amazing southern cooking, start here.

Makes 8 cups
6 cups water
1^1/$_4$ pounds corn grits
1 quart heavy cream
1 pound unsalted butter
2 tablespoons sea salt
2 tablespoons freshly ground pepper

Bring the water to boil in a large pot, with a whisk stir the water and grits together. Stir the grits for at least 5 minutes. Cover and simmer for about 3 hours, adding water whenever necessary, if grits appear dry. Slow cooking the

grits allows the water to absorb more completely and makes for a creamier grit. When grits are cooked add the heavy cream, butter, salt, and pepper, mixing until the ingredients are all combined and creamy. Serve warm.

TOMATO JAM

A surprising sauce; the acidity in it really uplifts any dish to which it is added. We have paired it with a pretty hearty dish of grits and smoked pork belly; the jam cuts through the fat and creates another flavor dimension. It's a can't-be-missed condiment.

Makes 2 cups
2 tablespoons olive oil
2 cloves garlic, crushed
1 tablespoons fresh ginger, grated
1 large red onion, small dice
$^1/_4$ cup honey
$^1/_4$ cup brown sugar
1 teaspoon ginger powder
$^1/_4$ teaspoon whole cloves
3 cinnamon sticks
3 star anise
3 cardamom seeds
5 large fresh tomatoes
$^1/_4$ cup brown ale
$^1/_4$ cup cider vinegar

In a medium saucepan heat the olive oil and add the garlic, fresh ginger, and red onions, and sauté until the onions become translucent. Add the honey, brown sugar, ginger powder, cloves, cinnamon sticks, star anise, and cardamom, sauté for 2 minutes and then add the tomatoes, vinegar, and beer.

Simmer the tomato mix for about 1 hour, stir occasionally. The tomatoes will begin to soften and the liquid will reduce. Remove the spice pods. Pour the tomato mix into the blender and puree.

SECTION PAGE
Smokin' Barbeque Menu 189

BEER BATTERED ONION RINGS

This tempura batter puts a nice crunchy, light coating on these giant rings. This batter will work with lighter beers, including pale ales, lagers, wheat beers, and IPAs.

Makes about 12 onion rings
$1/2$ cup beer
$1/2$ cup cold water
1 large egg yolk
2 tablespoons sesame oil
$1/3$ cup all-purpose flour
$1/8$ cup cornstarch
3 medium size white onions, wide slices
8 cups vegetable oil

Preheat fryer to 350 degrees. If you do not have a fryer, you can create a deep fryer with a large stockpot. Pour the oil into the pot and heat to 350 degrees.

Mix the dry ingredients in a medium bowl and set aside. Mix the wet ingredients in a medium bowl and set aside. Keep all wet ingredients in an ice bath with kosher salt at all times. It is essential that all the ingredients stay ice cold or else the batter will not puff up and crunch properly.

Dip the onion rings into the batter and let the excess drip off. Carefully place the battered onions into the hot oil one at a time. Fry until the onion rings begin to float and the batter is golden brown, about 3–5 minutes. Remove from the fryer onto a paper towel lined plate. Serve immediately.

SMOKED AND ROASTED RIBS

These ribs are tender, meaty, juicy and fall right off the bone. At our restaurant, they were nicknamed "the business man's ribs" because you could enjoy them while wearing your Sunday best without even picking up the bone.

Serves 4–6 people
2 racks pork spareribs
2 cups Gartrell's Dry Rub
1 cup water

Rub the ribs with 2 cups of Gartrell's Dry rub. Place them in a smoker at 180 degrees and cook for 2 hours. We prefer to smoke with oak wood but other smoking woods that we recommend are hickory, apple wood and mesquite. After the ribs have smoked remove them from the smoker and place thin into a large oven safe baking dish. Add 1 cup of water into the pan and wrap the whole pan all the way around with plastic wrap and then foil. Finish the ribs in a 300 degree oven for about 7 hours or until tender and falling off the bone. Remove and serve with Gartrell's Epic Beer barbeque sauce.

DRY RIB RUB

We rub this mix on our ribs and pulled pork before they are cooked and then finish with our wet beer barbeque sauce.

Makes 1 cup
6 tablespoons kosher salt
2 tablespoons black pepper
1 tablespoon cayenne pepper
2 tablespoons garlic, fresh and minced
2 tablespoons onion, fresh and minced
2 tablespoons paprika
1 tablespoon coriander, crushed
1 tablespoon fresh thyme
1 tablespoon fresh rosemary

Combine all the ingredients in a food processor until all combined. Spread the mix out on a cookie sheet in thin layer. Let dry completely, which usually takes about 24 hours. When the mix is dry, put in the food processor one more time, mix until the lumps are gone and all one size.

BROWN SUGAR AND COUNTRY HAM COLLARD GREENS

These collard greens are truly a labor of love for our chef Luther. This is not a quick dish to make, but it certainly is worth the effort and time invested.

Serves 4 people
2 bunches collards, washed and sliced into 1 inch pieces
1 smoked ham hock
8 cups water
1 teaspoon salt
1 teaspoon pepper
$^1/_2$ cup brown sugar

Place the ham hocks in a stockpot and cover with the water. Bring water to a boil on high heat and then turn down to medium heat and simmer until the ham hock completely falls off the bone, which will take about 3–4 hours. This ham stock will reduce to about 2 cups.

Put the collard greens into the stock and cover. Cook over medium heat, stirring often and cook for 3–4 hours, or until greens are tender. Add the salt, pepper, and brown sugar. We recommend serving it with pepper vinegar to taste.

SWEET ONION HUSHPUPPIES

A soft onion flavor enveloped in cornmeal. Cover these hushpuppies with honey butter and it does not get much better.

Make 15–20 hushpuppies
1 medium yellow onion, pureed
1 cup all-purpose flour
$1^1/_2$ cups corn meal
2 large whole eggs
2 tablespoons sugar
2 teaspoons salt
$^1/_2$ tablespoon pepper
2 tablespoons baking powder
$^1/_2$ cup whole milk

Preheat fryer to 350 degrees.
Combine all the ingredients in large bowl. Mix until batter is smooth. Let sit for 10 minutes. Spoon the batter carefully into the hot oil, one hushpuppy at a time. Do not overload your oil to prevent the oil from getting to cool and over saturating your hushpuppies. Cook until hushpuppies are golden brown about 4 minutes.

ROASTED OKRA

People may believe that okra is best fried, in soup, or pickled, but we have discovered the most delicious way to eat okra: ROASTED! This is a great vegetable to cook with dinner anytime.

Serves 4 people
1 pound fresh okra
Salt and pepper, to taste
2 tablespoons olive oil

Preheat oven to 425 degrees.

Wash the okra and place in medium bowl. Sprinkle the okra with salt, pepper, and the olive oil. Using a spatula stir the okra to coat all sides. Spread the okra in single layer on a sheet pan. Bake in the oven for about 8–10 minutes until okra starts to brown and become soft. Remove from sheet pan and serve hot.

PEACH CRISP

Fresh crisps are casual, delicious, and easy to make. Pick your peaches during peak picking season and you hardly need to use any sugar. This recipe can be translated to apples, berries, or plums.

Serves 4 people
4 peaches, cut in 8 pieces each
6 teaspoons Lambic beer
1 cup all-purpose flour
$^1/_2$ cup rolled oats
1 cup brown sugar
1 teaspoon cinnamon
1 cup unsalted butter, cut in small pieces
$^1/_2$ teaspoon sea salt
$^1/_4$ teaspoon ground black pepper

Preheat the oven to 350 degrees. Wash and cut the peaches into 8 pieces each, removing the pieces from the center seed. Place the peaches in large oven safe ramekins or an 8x8 inch baking pan. Put 1 tablespoon of beer in each ramekin or 4 tablespoons of beer in the large baking pan.

In a separate bowl combine the flour, oats, sugar, cinnamon, butter, salt, pepper, and 2 tablespoons beer. Mix until the butter pieces are about pea size. Sprinkle the mix over the peaches, distributing evenly amongst the ramekins. Bake the crisps for about 30 minutes or until the peaches are soft and the crust is browned. Serve warm with whipped cream or ice cream.

THE BEER WEDDING

Now we all know that the wedding is all about the bride, right? Well what about the groom? We propose a compromise. Flowers, decorations, and fanfare for the bride. Beer for the groom.

Over the years we have catered countless weddings, rehearsal dinners, and after-wedding brunches. But when a couple comes to us united by their love of beer, we can't wait to help them create their menu. And we find that the guests love it. After all, who is going to complain about being offered a caramelized, bacon-y, pine nut filled date paired with a tiny glass of one of the best IPA in the world? Or pan-seared salmon paired with Imperial Pilsner? And of course, the piece-de-resistance, a milk stout ice cream wedding cake!

BEER WEDDING MENU
Cocktail hour:

BLACK FOREST BACON WRAPPED DATES STUFFED WITH UNION JACK IPA PINE NUT BUTTER
Union Jack IPA, Firestone Walker Brewing Company, California

SMOKED BEEF TARTAR WITH LEMON ZEST, RED ONION, CAPERS, BEER INFUSED MUSTARD SEEDS, AND CRISPY SHAVED POTATOES
Rauch ür Bock, Caldera Brewing Company, Oregon

ZUCCHINI, CORN, HERB FRITTERS WITH GARTRELL'S CREAMY MUSTARD SAUCE AND PEPPER JELLY DIPPING SAUCE
Rare Vos Amber Ale, Ommegang Brewery, New York

3 COURSE PLATED
1st Course
    Caprese Salad with organic heirloom tomatoes and basil, fresh buffalo mozzarella, farmhouse balsamic vinaigrette
    Brooklyn Sorachi Ace, Brooklyn Brewery, New York
2nd Course
    Pan-Seared Salmon with shallot and rosemary gratin potatoes, green beans, imperial pilsner buerre blanc
    Morimoto Imperial Pilsner, Rogue Ales, Oregon
3rd Course
    Milk Stout Ice Cream Wedding Cake
    Milk Stout Nitro, Left Hand Brewery, Colorado

FEATURED BEERS

UNION JACK IPA

Made by: Firestone Walker Brewing Company
Style: American IPA
From: California
7.5% ABV
Serve in a tulip glass

This is a medium copper-gold beer with a white head. This beer brings the strong bitter grapefruit and is balanced with light piney, herbal essence, light honeyed graham cracker sweetness, and tropical fruits. This beer pairs well with fatty meats, pine nuts, citrus desserts, and salads.

RAUCH ÜR BOCK

Made by: Caldera Brewing Company
Style: Rauchbier
From: Oregon
7.4% ABV
Serve in a dimple glass

This beer pours a nice copper with ruby-red highlights. This beer has a bold smoky flavor with barely-there bitter hop notes. This beer has light toasted malt sweetness and meaty flavors. This beer pairs well with red meat, creamy rich dishes, and barbeque.

RARE VOS AMBER ALE

Made by: Ommegang Brewery
Style: Belgian Pale Ale
From: New York
6.5% ABV
Serve in a beer Trappist glass

This beer pours a hazy amber color with a creamy head. This beer is smooth and mellow with subtle caramel and citrus flavors. It pairs well with pub foods, seafood, and barbeque.

SORACHI ACE
Made by: Brooklyn Brewery
Style: Farmhouse ale
From: New York
7.6% ABV
Serve in a tulip

This beer pours a hazy straw color with a big, dense, white head. The flavor is clean, clear, and dry with citrus, lemongrass, peppercorn, and a light bready malt. This beer pairs well with fish, cheese, and salads.

MORIMOTO IMPERIAL PILSNER
Made by: Rogue Ale
Style: Imperial Pilsner
From: Oregon
8.8% ABV
Serve in a footed pilsner

This beer pours golden honey in color with a nice white head. The flavors are herbaceous, lemongrass, citrusy hops, and a malty sweet backbone. This beer pairs well with fish, chicken, and salads.

MILK STOUT NITRO
Made by: Left Hand Brewing Company
Style: Milk Stout
From: Colorado
6% ABV
Serve in a pint glass

This beer pours dark chocolate in color with a thick creamy head developing from the nitrogen bubbles. This beer tastes like whipped cream, roasted coffee, and milk chocolate with a slightly bitter backbone. This beer is made for desserts, and it pairs well with chocolate, coffee, and vanilla. It would also work well in barbeque sauces and stews.

RECIPES

BLACK FOREST BACON-WRAPPED DATES FILLED WITH PINE NUT BUTTER

These dates are a little more work than your typical bacon-wrapped date, but it is worth every minute spent. These dates are sweet, caramelized and bacon-y. The beer marinade and pine nut butter add a piney flavor that completely balances out this fantastic bite. We recommend making more of these than you think you need, because once you have one you will keep coming back for these savory little bites.

Serves 6 people
18 large dates, pitted
$1/2$ cup pine nuts, toasted
2 cups + 2 tablespoons IPA beer
$1/8$ teaspoon sea salt and pepper
6 pieces thick cut bacon
18 toothpicks

Combine the toasted pine nuts, 2 tablespoons IPA beer, salt, and pepper into a Cuisinart or blender. Blend until the pine nuts become butter and resemble almond butter. Place the pine nut butter into a piping bag with a small round tip. If you do not have a piping back a Ziploc bag with the corner cut off will work. Fill each pitted date with the pine nut butter. After all the dates are filled, refrigerate for 30 minutes to allow the filling to firm up.

Cut the bacon into thirds getting 18 even pieces. Remove the dates from the refrigerator and wrap them with the bacon pieces, securing the bacon with a toothpick. Place your dates in a small but deep dish and cover them with 2 cups of cold IPA, marinate the bacon dates for about 1 hour. Remove them from beer and discard the beer marinade, cook the dates for about 12 minutes at 425 degrees. They should be golden brown and the bacon should be fully cooked. Best served warm.

SMOKED BEEF TARTAR

This is a traditional tartar with a twist. We have served these up in beautiful little glass dishes for passed hors d'oeuvres at parties or portioned up a larger serving to start a meal at the table. Either way this is a light, fun, and delicious dish to be enjoyed with a great smoky beer.

Serves 6 people

3 tablespoons mustard seeds

4 ounces smoked beer

12 ounces beef tenderloin

Salt and pepper, to taste

2 whole egg yolks, preferably organic, fresh and local

6 small red bliss potatoes, shaved into small pieces

4 cups vegetable oil

$1/2$ teaspoon fresh parsley, fine chop

$1/2$ teaspoon fresh chives, fine chop

2 tablespoons lemon zest

2 tablespoons red onion, fine dice

2 tablespoons capers

Start with your mustard seeds. Bring 4 ounces of beer to a simmer and add your mustard seeds, then remove them from the heat and let the seeds soak, covered overnight. Then they are ready to serve. Use any extra liquid that does not absorb as a little extra sauce.

Pick your tenderloin from a good source that carried very fresh, high quality meat. Salt and pepper the tenderloin and place it in a smoker for about $1^{1}/_{2}$ hours at 190 degrees. This process infuses the meat with the nice smoky flavor without cooking it. We prefer to smoke with oak wood, but other smoking woods that we recommend are hickory, applewood, and mesquite. Remove the meat from the smoker and refrigerate for 30 minutes.

To make the shaved potatoes, clean the potatoes and with the skin on, cut the potatoes into super thin, shaved pieces and soak them in cold water for 15–20 minutes. After they have soaked, drain the potatoes and pat dry. Bring your vegetable oil up to 340 degrees in a large pot. Fry the potato shavings for 45 second to 1 minute, they will cook very quickly. Remove when they are golden brown. Salt, pepper, and sprinkle with finely chopped herbs immediately. Serve while fresh and warm.

When ready to serve this dish, grind your beef up with a grinder or food processor, add the egg yolks, salt, and pepper, mix together and serve on the side with the shaved potatoes, mustard seeds, lemon zest, onion, and capers.

ZUCCHINI, CORN, AND HERB FRITTERS

Delicate puffs served with sweet pepper jelly—always a hit.

Makes 18 fritters

1$^1/_4$ cups all-purpose flour
1 teaspoon salt
$^1/_2$ teaspoon pepper
1$^1/_2$ teaspoons baking powder
$^1/_4$ cup whole milk
2 tablespoons amber ale
2 whole eggs
2$^1/_2$ teaspoons unsalted butter, melted
1$^1/_2$ teaspoons garlic, finely chopped
4 tablespoons grainy mustard
$^3/_4$ cup zucchini, grated
$^1/_2$ cup fresh corn, cut off the cob
$^1/_2$ cup chives, finely chopped
$^1/_4$ cup parsley, finely chopped
$^1/_2$ gallon vegetable oil

Husk the corn and cut the kernel off the cob. In a sauté pan cook the corn covered with 1 teaspoon of butter for 5–7 minutes or until the corn is soft, cool and set aside.

Combine the flour, salt, pepper, and baking powder in a mixing bowl. In a separate bowl combine the milk, beer, eggs, 1$^1/_2$ teaspoons butter, mustard, garlic, zucchini, corn, parsley, and chives, mix well. Add the wet ingredients to the dry ingredients and mix until just combined.

Preheat the vegetable oil in a large pot to 350 degrees. Drop the batter a tablespoon at a time into hot oil cook for about 3–5 minutes or until they are golden brown and the center comes out clean when checked with a toothpick. Serve hot with pepper jelly and Gartrell's creamy mustard sauce.

RED PEPPER JELLY

This is a very versatile recipe. We use it as a dipping sauce with fritters and fried shrimp. It complements cheese well and can even be used on burgers or chicken.

Makes 2 cups

3 red bell peppers
1 cup sugar
$^3/_4$ cup cider vinegar
$^1/_4$ cup lemon juice
$^1/_4$ ounce pectin
3 tablespoons amber, hefeweizen, or pilsner beer

Remove the stem and seeds from the peppers, roughly chop them, and then pulse them in the Cuisinart until they are in small pieces. Place all the ingredients, except for the pectin, in saucepan and simmer for 15 minutes. Add the pectin and simmer for 3 minutes more. Remove from heat and add the beer. Refrigerate the sauce to cool. This sauce can be stored for up to 2 weeks in the refrigerator.

CAPRESE SALAD

Make this salad in the heart of summer when the heirloom tomatoes are plump and falling off the vines. Heirloom tomatoes are truly a special vegetable, they are so vibrant and comprised of so many colors and flavors. We like to use a variety of different heirloom tomatoes for this dish. Some of our favorites are Brandywine, green zebra, yellow sunray, black cherries, and Mr. Stripy. Find what is the best at your farmer's market and use those.

Serves 6 people

2 Brandywine tomatoes, thick slices
2 Mr. Stripy tomatoes, thick slices
4 green zebra tomatoes, thick slices
4 yellow sunray tomatoes, thick slices
12 black cherry tomatoes, quartered
6 ounces buffalo mozzarella, thick slices
36 pieces basil
4–6 tablespoons farmhouse balsamic vinaigrette
1 baguette, sliced and toasted

Slice all the tomatoes with a sharp knife; be sure to slice the tomatoes so each plate gets equal amounts of each tomato. Slice the mozzarella. Arrange the tomato slices on the plate(s) alternating with the mozzarella and basil. Drizzle the vinaigrette over the arranged tomatoes and cheese. Serve with freshly toasted baguette and a cold farmhouse ale.

FARMHOUSE BALSAMIC VINAIGRETTE

Our twist on a simple but delicious dressing. This dressing is paired with our Caprese salad, but can be used on any salad.

Makes 1 $^3/_4$ cups

$^1/_2$ cup aged balsamic vinegar
$^1/_4$ cup farmhouse ale
1 cup extra virgin olive oil
2 teaspoons honey
$^1/_4$ teaspoon sea salt
$^1/_4$ teaspoon fresh ground pepper

Combine all ingredients in a blender except the oil. Blend the ingredients until completely combined. Add the oil in a steady stream until all incorporated. Serve on salad, may be stored for up to 1 week.

PAN-SEARED SALMON

This is a great way to enjoy salmon, get a nice golden crust on the outside while still keeping the fish moist and tender on the inside.

Serves 6 people

6 6-ounce salmon filets
6 tablespoons olive oil
Sea salt and pepper

Season the salmon with salt and pepper on both sides. In a hot sauté pan add the oil, carefully place the salmon pretty side down in the pan, sear the salmon for about $2\frac{1}{2}$ minutes on one side and flip over, cook for another $2\frac{1}{2}$ minutes. Serve immediately.

SHALLOT AND ROSEMARY GRATIN POTATOES

These gratin potatoes are so creamy and good. Use them as a side dish for any meal.

Serves 12–15 people

3 sprigs rosemary
14 garlic cloves, crushed
3 cups olive oil
5 pounds red skin potatoes
3 large shallots
1 quart heavy cream
1 teaspoon salt and pepper

In a food processor, combine the rosemary, garlic, salt, pepper, and 1 cup of olive oil and puree until the mix is smooth. Remove the mix from the processor and wash. Then slice the potatoes and shallots on a 2 millimeter blade in the food processor. If you don't have a food processor use a mandolin or a knife, the main goal is to slice the potato very thin and a consistent thickness.

Mix the potatoes and shallots, sauté them in a large hot skillet with 2 cups olive oil until the potatoes begin to get some light browning color. Combine the rosemary mixture with the potatoes in the skillet and cook for 5 minutes, stirring often. Add $\frac{1}{2}$ the cream and cook for 4 minutes, stirring often. Add the rest of the cream, and pour the potato mix into a 9 x 13 inch baking pan, cover with foil, and cook in 350 degree oven for about 45 minutes.

MILK STOUT ICE CREAM CAKE

Homemade ice cream is one of the most decadent, rich things you can make for yourself, so why not make it big and assemble it into a cake for birthdays, anniversaries, or weddings. Luther and I have eaten ice cream cake every year on our birthdays since we can remember. Making beer ice cream has really put new life into how we see ice cream cake. This cake can be made with different beers, but we recommend sticking with the stout or porter category.

Makes 1 8-inch layered cake

3 cups chocolate cookie crumbs, see page 28
6 cups milk stout ice cream
2 cups dark chocolate ganache, see page 14
1 cup milk stout caramel sauce

Assemble the cake in a frozen 8 inch deep cake ring or 8 inch deep cake pan, the ring will be easier to remove later, but the pan will work fine as well. Line the bottom of the cake pan with parchment paper. Spread half the cookie crumbs on the bottom of the pan and pat them flat to form a crust. Pour 1 cup of ganache over the cookie base and spread it evenly. Drizzle $1/3$ cup of caramel sauce over the ganache. Freeze this base for 30 minutes. After the base has firmed up spread 3 cups of stout ice cream evenly over the base in the pan. Depend-ing on how firm your ice cream is you may need to return the cake to the freezer for another 30 minutes. If your ice cream is pretty firm you can skip the freezer and proceed to the next layer. Spread the remaining cookie crumbs on ice cream layer, spread 1 cup of ganache over crumbs, and drizzle $1/3$ cup caramel sauce. Freeze for 30 minutes. When chocolate layer is firm spread the last 3 cups of ice cream evenly on the 2nd chocolate layer. Drizzle with last bit of caramel and freeze until solid. Serve.

MILK STOUT ICE CREAM

Beer ice cream is the most pleasant surprise we have discovered in the years of pairing beer with food. The combination of cream and sweet balances perfectly with the beer flavors malty and bitter. This ice cream is luscious and flavorful; you will find yourself craving this unique treat. We have used it in an ice cream cake, but by all means eat it in its own, it's that good.

Makes 8 cups
4 cups heavy whipping cream
$1^1/_2$ cups milk stout beer
1 tablespoon vanilla
$1^1/_2$ cups sugar
Pinch of salt
12 egg yolks

Combine the heavy cream, beer, vanilla, half the sugar, and a pinch of salt in a medium saucepan. Bring mixture just to a simmer and remove from heat.

In a separate medium bowl whisk the egg yolks and the rest of the sugar until all combined. Gradually temper the warm cream mixture into the egg mix. Add the warm cream 1 ladle at a time whisking constantly until all cream is combined with eggs. Return to the pot and cook over medium heat, stirring constantly, until it becomes thick enough to coat the back of a wooden spoon. This takes about 3 minutes. Strain ice cream base through a fine chinois into a medium bowl set over a bowl of ice; let cool, stirring occasionally. When ice cream base is cool, process the base in an ice cream maker according to manufacturer's instructions. Store in airtight container in your freezer.

STOUT CARAMEL SAUCE

This is a perfect sauce for dipping, drizzling, or adding to cake or desserts.

Makes 2 cups
1 cup sugar
$1/_4$ cup light corn syrup
2 tablespoons water
6 tablespoons butter
$1/_4$ cup beer
$1/_2$ cup heavy cream

Combine the sugar, corn syrup, and water in a medium saucepot. Be sure your pot is very clean, free of any grease or dirt. Carefully wipe the inside sides of the pot with a wet pastry brush to be sure there is no extra sugar on the sides.

Cook the sugar mix until it reaches a dark amber color, which will take about 10 minutes. Do not stir the sugar while it is cooking.

When the desired color had been reached turn the heat off and add the butter a little at a time. The butter will react with the hot sugar, so be careful that it does not boil over or burn you. Stir the butter with a wooden spoon until the bubbling goes down, and add the cream a little at a time until it is all combined. Finish the sauce with the beer. Stir until combined. Serve this sauce warm.

AUTUMN

Autumn brings turning leaves—sprinkling the landscape with bright reds, yellows, and orange. The air becomes crisp and fresh, the temperatures lending themselves to outdoor festivals, visits to breweries and local orchards. We love autumn and the comforting foods that come with it. The menus in this section focus on juicy apples from the orchard and squash, pumpkins, and hearty root vegetables. Our beer choices are light and fresh hard ciders, German Märzen's, Brown Ales, and warming Strong Ales.

AUTUMN CELEBRATION

Fall is a time that we enjoy the bright colors of the turning leaves, the crisp cool air, and the warm scents coming from the kitchen. To us this menu really represents comfort food in autumn. We have included the aromatic scents of caramelized onions and warm biscuits. The luscious apple flavors straight from the orchard and fried corn bread chicken paired with a sweet and hopped hard cider. To finish off this decadent meal we have created a crème brulee around a fantastic peanut butter porter. We hope that these dishes bring you as much comfort as they do us.

AUTUMN CELEBRATION MENU

1st Course

Caramelized Onion Soup with cheddar biscuits

Indian Brown Ale, Dogfish Head Brewery, Delaware

2nd Course

Fried Cornbread Encrusted Chicken with Anthem hard cider cream sauce, red bliss smashed potatoes, and peas

Anthem Hops Hard Cider, Wandering Aengus Ciderworks, Oregon

3rd Course

Roasted Peanut Butter Crème Brule with flourless dark chocolate cookies

Sweet Baby Jesus American Porter, DuClaw Brewing Company, Maryland

FEATURED BEERS

INDIAN BROWN ALE

Made by: Dogfish Head Brewery

Style: American Brown Ale

From: Delaware

7.2% ABV

Serve in a dimpled mug or pint glass

This beer pours dark brown with a hearty tan head. It is a cross between a Scottish ale, IPA, and American Brown ale. The taste is nutty, brown sugar, bitter espresso, and roasted malts that lead to a bitter hops finish. This beer pairs well with roasted, braised, and smoked meats, caramelized onions, stews, prosciutto, chocolate, and coffee desserts.

ANTHEM HOPS HARD CIDER

Made by: Wandering Aengus Ciderworks

Style: Hard Cider

From: Oregon

6.5% ABV

Serve in a flute or lager glass

This beer pours a very pale bond color with basically not head. It tastes of sweet fermented apples with hints of citrus, floral hop bitterness. This beer pairs well with chicken, apples, and salads.

SWEET BABY JESUS AMERICAN PORTER

Made by: DuClaw Brewing Company

Style: American Porter

From: Maryland

6.5% ABV

Serve in an English pint

This beer pours a deep dark brown with a think tan head. It comes on strong with peanut butter, bitter cocoa, and roasted malts. Peanut butter flavor lingers in the palate. This beer pairs with stews and roasted meats, peanut butter, and chocolate.

RECITES

RECIPES

CARAMELIZED ONION SOUP WITH CHEDDAR BISCUIT

This soup is warm, filling and a twist on a classic comfort food. We have decided to add a super cheesy cheddar biscuit on top instead of the traditional melted cheese. We have paired this recipe with an Indian Brown Ale because the dark caramelized flavors in the beer and the bitter finish really complements the sweet caramelized flavors in this soup.

Makes 8 cups

6 tablespoons unsalted butter

2 pounds sweet yellow onions, peeled and thinly sliced

2 pounds red onions, peeled and thinly sliced

2 bay leaves

2 sprigs of fresh thyme

1 teaspoon sea salt

1 tablespoon all-purpose flour

3 cups beef broth

1 teaspoon fresh ground pepper

$1/2$ cup beer

In a large heavy bottomed pan melt the butter over medium-low heat. Add the thinly sliced onions to the pan in a thin, even layer. Add the bay leaves and thyme. Stir the onions and herbs to coat with the butter. Cover and cook for 15 minutes, stirring occasionally. After 15 minutes remove the cover and continue cooking over medium-low heat stirring occasionally for about 45 minutes or until the onions are a dark caramel color.

Stir in the salt and flour to coat the onions. Add the beef broth and pepper. Cook for 30 minutes over medium heat. Finish the soup by adding $1/2$ cup of beer and cook for 10 more minutes. Serve with our cheddar biscuit.

FRIED CORNBREAD ENCRUSTED CHICKEN

This recipe is a family favorite. It has graced our menu at the restaurant many times over the years and is always a big hit. The combination of fried chicken, fresh apple cream sauce, and hard cider is brilliant. We usually serve this dish with smashed potatoes.

Serves 6

1 medium yellow onion, pureed

1 cup all-purpose flour

$1 1/2$ cups corn meal

2 large whole eggs

2 tablespoons sugar

2 teaspoons salt

$1/2$ tablespoon pepper

2 tablespoons baking powder

$1/2$ cup milk

6 pieces chicken, thighs and legs

1 gallon vegetable oil

Combine all the ingredients except the chicken in a large bowl. Mix until batter is smooth. Refrigerate for 1 hour. Score the chicken by slicing the top of the thigh and leg with a knife about $1/4$ inch deep. Slice diagonal lines and then slice lines in the other direction to form diamond shapes.

Preheat 1 gallon of oil to 340 degrees in a large, deep pot.

When the oil is the proper temperature dip the chicken in the cornbread batter and carefully place in the hot oil. Fry the chicken until it has an internal temperature of 165 degrees or about 8–10 minutes. Remove the chicken from the fryer and serve with Apple Cider Cream Sauce.

APPLE CIDER CREAM SAUCE

This sauce is a perfect cold weather sauce. It is rich, creamy, and filled with apple sweetness. We pair this sauce with our fried chicken and Hard Cider.

Serves 6

2 tablespoons unsalted butter

2 apples, peeled, cored and sliced

1 cup apple cider

4 cups hard cider

2 tablespoons grainy mustard

2 cups heavy cream

Salt and pepper to taste

In a medium size sauté pan melt the butter and sauté the apples for 1 minute. Add the apple cider and the hard cider to the pan. Reduce over medium heat until the cider mix becomes a thick syrup. Stir in the mustard and heavy cream. Reduce the mix by $1/4$ over medium heat. Salt and pepper to taste and serve warm over friend chicken.

CHEDDAR BEER BISCUIT

These biscuits are perfect on their own. They are soft, fluffy, and moist. Serve them warm with our onion soup.

Makes 12 $2^1/2$ inch biscuits

2 cups all-purpose flour

2 teaspoons baking powder

$1/4$ teaspoon baking soda

1 teaspoon sea salt

1 teaspoon fresh ground pepper

4 teaspoons fresh chives, small dice (optional)

$1/2$ cup butter, cut in small slices and frozen

$3/4$ cup buttermilk

$1/4$ cup beer

2 cups cheddar cheese, grated

Preheat oven to 425 degrees. Grease a baking sheet.

Combine the flour, baking powder, baking soda, salt, pepper, and chives in a medium sized bowl.

Cut the frozen butter pieces into the dry ingredients, mix until the butter is pea sized and dough looks like course sand. Combine $1/2$ cup buttermilk and the beer.

Add the buttermilk mix into the flour-butter mix. Mix to just combine the ingredients and pour out of the bowl onto a floured surface. Knead the dough until it comes together, about 3 minutes of kneading. Be sure not to overdo it, the butter should still be about pea size.

Roll the dough out to $1/2$ inch thickness and cut with a cookie cutter to desired size and shape and place on greased baking sheet. At this point you can chose to bake the biscuits without the cheese or if you are adding cheese refrigerate the cut out biscuits for 1 hour to firm the dough up. When biscuits are firm, cut the biscuits in half horizontally and insert 1 tablespoon of grated cheddar cheese and seal the cheese in the middle of the 2 halves of the biscuit.

Brush the leftover buttermilk on the top of the biscuits, sprinkle with salt and pepper and split the remaining cheese between the biscuits and coat the tops. Bake in the oven for 15–20 minutes or until golden brown.

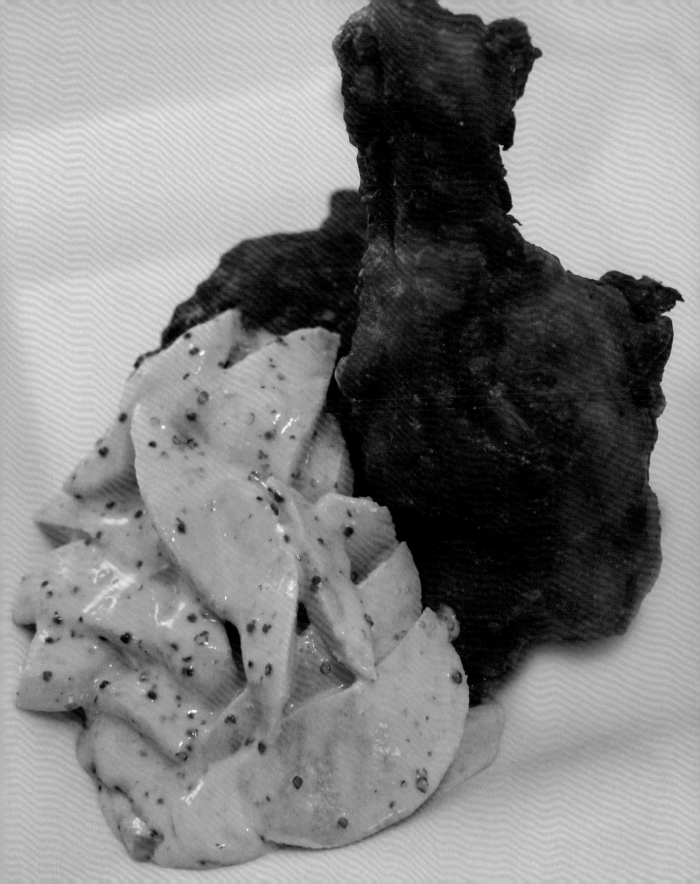

PEANUT BUTTER CRÈME BRULEE

If you are a peanut butter fan then this is the dessert for you. It is creamy, savory, and sweet. Add a chocolate cookie to create a peanut butter cup effect.

Serves 8

3 cups heavy cream
$^1/_2$ cup beer
1 teaspoon vanilla
$^1/_2$ teaspoon sea salt
1 cup peanut butter
1 cup sugar
8 egg yolks

Preheat the oven to 300 degrees.

In a medium saucepan bring the heavy cream, beer, vanilla, and salt to a simmer.

In a separate bowl whisk together the egg yolks and $^1/_2$ cup of sugar. When the cream mix is hot, remove it from the heat and whisk in the peanut butter. The peanut butter will slowly melt into the mix and the cream will become smooth. When the peanut butter is fully combined in the mix temper the cream mix into the egg yolks and sugar one ladle at a time whisking constantly until all the cream is incorporated into the eggs.

Place the crème brulee molds in a deep-sided pan like a cake pan or roasting pan. Divide the custard evenly between the crème brulee molds and pour hot water into the roasting pan, fill the pan so the water is half way up the molds. Bake for about 40–45 minutes or until just set, they should tremble slightly in the center when lightly shaken. Remove from the water bath and refrigerate for a minimum of 2 hours. It is best for the crème brulee to be cold and completely set up before serving.

When ready to serve, divide the remaining $^1/_2$ cup of sugar between the custard cups, spread the sugar evenly on the tops of the crème brule, and using a torch carefully melt the sugar in an even layer on the brulee, being careful to keep the torch moving to avoid burning the sugar. Serve.

FLOURLESS DARK CHOCOLATE COOKIES

If you enjoy chocolate, then these cookies are sure to hit the spot. We love to serve them warm with the chocolate centers melting, but they are delicious at any temperature.

Makes 30 Cookies

2 cups dark chocolate chips
4 egg whites
3 cups powdered sugar
$^1/_2$ cup cocoa powder
1 $^1/_2$ tablespoons cornstarch
$^1/_4$ teaspoon salt
$^1/_4$ cup porter or stout

Preheat the oven to 400 degrees and grease baking pan.

Melt 1 cup of chocolate chips in a double boiler. While chocolate is melting separate your eggs and beat in a mixer with the whisk attachment until the whites reach soft peak, slightly stiff but not standing straight up, they fold back into themselves. When whites reach soft peaks, slowly add 1$^1/_2$ cups powdered sugar and continue mixing until the whites reach medium peak, the peaks will be more firm than the soft peaks and will hold longer but will not stand up straight.

In a separate bowl combine 1 cup powdered sugar, cocoa powder, cornstarch, and salt. Fold the whipped eggs into the dry ingredients until the dry ingredients just are incorporated into the egg mix, but be careful to not over mix. Stir in the melted chocolate and remaining chocolate chips.

Roll the cookie dough into 1 inch round balls and roll in the remaining $^1/_2$ cup of powdered sugar. Bake in the oven for 10 minutes and serve warm.

HARVEST DINNER

Fall brings with it so many special ingredients, and with the change in weather, appetites turn to hearty, comforting food. This menu feels like a fall celebration to us, from the spiced butternut squash salad with lentils and creamy goat cheese to the seared duck breasts with a black currant reduction and the warm finish of delightful apple fritters with Bohemian Cider ice cream. We have paired this menu with beers that really add to the flavors of the food. These beers really bring out the flavor profile of each one of these dishes.

HARVEST DINNER MENU
1st Course
  Spiced Butternut Squash Salad with lentils, goat cheese, roasted squash seeds, arugula, blood orange vinaigrette
  Double IPA Brewmaster Series, Longtrail Brewing Company, Vermont
2nd Course
  Seared Duck Breast with black currant-beer reduction sauce and parsnip-carrot puree
  Lindemans Cassis Lambic, Brouwerij Lindemans, Belgium
3rd Course
  Apple Fritters with Bohemian Cider Ice Cream
  Crispin Bohemian Artisanal Reserve Hard Cider, Crispin Cidery, California

FEATURED BEERS

DOUBLE IPA BREWMASTERS SERIES
Made by: Longtrail Brewing Company
Style: Imperial IPA
From: Vermont
8.6% ABV
Serve in a snifter

This beer pours hazy dark amber with a thick off-white head. The taste is a strong bready, malty caramel up front with strong grapefruit hops. In the end the beer begins to balance with flavors of pine and floral hops that balance out the malty sweetness perfectly. This beer pairs well with salads, fried foods, chicken, and fruit desserts.

LINDEMANS CASSIS
Made by: Brouwerij Lindemans
Style: Lambic
From: Belgium
3.5% ABV
Serve in a stemmed Glass

This beer pours dark ruby with a frothy brown head. The flavor is strong, sweet black currant with a light mustiness with some sour notes. This beer pairs well with duck, dark fruits, and dessert.

BOHEMIAN
Made by: Crispin Cider Company
Style: Hard Cider
From: California
5.8% ABV
Serve in a lager glass

This beer pours a hazy burnt orange color. It is made with pilsner lager yeast and tastes like unfiltered apple cider, with hints of honey, citrus, and green apple. This beer pairs well with desserts, chicken, and salads.

RECIPES

SPICED BUTTERNUT SQUASH SALAD

This is a favorite salad of ours. It makes for a great vegetarian dish as well. This salad is hearty, spicy with earthy sweetness from the roasted squash.

Serves 6 people
6 ounces dry green lentils
18 ounces water
$1/2$ cup white onion, small dice
1 garlic clove, crushed
1 bay leaf
8 whole peppercorns
$1/2$ teaspoon sea salt

1 large butternut squash, peeled and cut into medium dice
$1/4$ cup olive oil
$1/2$ teaspoon cumin powder
$1/4$ teaspoon cayenne pepper

Sea salt and pepper to taste
3 ounces goat cheese
6 cups arugula
3 ounces Imperial blood orange vinaigrette

Mix together the lentils, water, onion, bay leaf, peppercorns, garlic, and salt in a medium pot. Simmer the lentils for 15–20 minutes or until tender but not mushy. Drain the lentils and set aside in a bowl.

Preheat the oven to 425 degrees. Peel, remove the seeds and cut the squash into a medium dice. Toss the squash pieces in a bowl with $1/4$ cup olive oil, cumin, cayenne pepper, salt, and pepper until all coated. Spread the squash out evenly on a baking sheet. Bake the squash pieces for about 10–12 minutes or until they are soft. Remove from the oven and set aside to cool slightly.

Reserve the seeds. Wash the seeds in warm water until clean, pat dry and toss them in the left over oil, spice mix in the bowl. Spread the seeds on a different baking sheet. Bake the seeds in the oven for 5–6 minutes or until they are golden brown, Remove the seeds and set aside.

In a large salad bowl add the arugula, gently mix the vinaigrette, lentils, and squash together with the arugula. Sprinkle the goat cheese on the salad and serve. This salad is at its best when it is room temperature. Enjoy with a nice imperial IPA.

IMPERIAL BLOOD ORANGE VINAIGRETTE

This is a slightly bitter orange vinaigrette that we serve with the spiced butternut squash salad. This vinaigrette is especially nice on a sweeter salad as it helps balance out the flavors.

Makes about 1$1/2$ cups
1 shallot, fine diced
Juice of 4 blood oranges
2 tablespoons honey
1 blood orange, zested

Juice of 1 lemon
$1/3$ cup Imperial IPA
1 teaspoon sea salt and pepper
1 cup extra virgin olive oil

Combine all ingredients in a blender except the oil. Blend the ingredients until completely combined and chopped. Add the oil in a steady stream until all incorporated. May be stored for up to 1 week.

SEARED DUCK BREAST WITH BLACK CURRANT LAMBIC REDUCTION

My sister tells me that Luther's duck has ruined her for any other.

Serves 6 people
16 ounces Cassis Lambic beer
1 tablespoon dried currants
$^1/_2$ cup veal demi-glace
6 duck breasts
3 tablespoons olive oil
Salt and pepper to taste

In a small sauce pot, combine the beer and currants; reduce the beer over low heat until it equals about half a cup. Mix in half a cup of demi-glace and set aside in a warm area.

Cut 3 shallow lines in fatty side of the duck breasts to score them. (Be sure not to cut too deep. You do not want to cut all the way to the meat.) Toss the breasts in the oil, salt, and pepper. Place the duck in a large, cold sauté pan, skin side down. Render the fat over medium-low heat until the fat becomes crunchy; this takes about 12–15 minutes. Turn the breasts over and cook for 1 minute more. Remove them from the heat, let them rest for a few minutes and slice. Serve with the Lambic reduction.

PARSNIP CARROT PUREE

This is a great side dish during the cool months. It's a nice alternative to potatoes, with a hearty, slightly spicy bite of horseradish.

Serves 6–8 people
8 parsnips, peeled, medium dice
3 carrots, peeled, medium dice
$^1/_4$ cup horseradish, peeled, grated
$^1/_2$ cup white onion, medium dice
2 teaspoons sea salt
1 teaspoon pepper
$^1/_2$ cup heavy cream
$^1/_2$ cup unsalted butter, melted

Bring 6 cups of water and 1 teaspoon of salt to a boil. Add the carrots, parsnip, horseradish, and onion. Boil the vegetables until they are tender; about 30 minutes. While vegetables are cooking, melt the butter and warm the cream in a small pan. When vegetables are cooked, strain them and allow to cool slightly. Place them in a blender. Pulse the vegetables and add the cream, butter, salt, and pepper. Puree the mix until completely smooth.

APPLE FRITTERS

These fritters are warm, sweet, and full of apple goodness. Serve them for dessert topped with ice cream or make them a special breakfast treat dusted with powdered sugar.

Makes 1 dozen

2 large apples, peeled and grated
$1/2$ cup whole milk
$1/4$ cup honey
$1/4$ cup hard cider
1 teaspoon vanilla
2 eggs
1 lemon, zested
2 cups all-purpose flour
$3/4$ cups brown sugar
1 teaspoon cinnamon
$1/2$ teaspoon cloves
$1/2$ teaspoon nutmeg
$1/2$ teaspoon sea salt
2 teaspoons baking powder
6 cups vegetable oil

Peel and grate the apples and set aside. In a small bowl, whisk together the milk, honey, cider, lemon zest, eggs and vanilla. In a separate medium size bowl, combine the sugar, flour, spices, salt and baking powder. Whisk the wet ingredients into the dry ingredients; mix until the batter is smooth. Add the grated apples and mix.

Pour the oil into a large, thick bottomed skillet; heat the oil to about 340 degrees. When the oil is hot, spoon the batter into the oil and fry for about 2 minutes or until they are golden brown. Flip and cook for another 2 minutes or until they are golden brown on all sides. Remove from the oil and serve hot.

CARAMELIZED APPLE CIDER ICE CREAM

The caramelized apple puree really enhances the already creamy texture. Serve this ice cream on its own or with hot apple fritters.

Makes 10 cups

3 apples, peeled, cored and medium dice
1$^1/_2$ cups Hard Apple cider
1 tablespoon vanilla
$^1/_4$ cup honey
1 lemon, zested
$^1/_4$ teaspoon cinnamon
$^1/_4$ teaspoon nutmeg
$^1/_4$ teaspoon sea salt
4 cups heavy cream
1$^1/_2$ cups sugar
12 egg yolks

In a saucepan, combine the apples, $^1/_2$ cup hard cider, vanilla, honey, lemon zest, cinnamon, nutmeg, and salt. Cook until the apples are soft, stir and cook until the apples begin to caramelize slightly. When apples are cooked, place them in a blender and add the remainder of the hard cider. Puree the apples and beer until the mix becomes smooth.

Bring the heavy cream to a simmer in a medium pot and remove from heat. In a separate medium bowl, whisk the egg yolks and the sugar until all combined. Gradually temper the warm cream mixture into the egg mix by adding the warm cream one ladle at a time, whisking constantly until all cream is combined with eggs.

Return to the pot and cook over medium heat, stirring constantly, until it becomes thick enough to coat the back of a wooden spoon; this takes about 3 minutes. Strain ice cream base through a fine chinois into a medium bowl. Whisk the apple cider puree into the cream base and set over a bowl of ice. Let cool, stirring occasionally. When ice cream base is cool, process the base in an ice cream maker according to manufacturer's instructions. Store in airtight container in your freezer.

OKTOBERFEST PARTY

Oktoberfest is celebrated around the world, but its epicenter is Munich Germany. Lasting 16 days from the end of September to the first week of October, it is the biggest party in the world celebrating beer, food, and friendship. We have had an annual Oktoberfest Celebration in our restaurant every year. We have included our favorite recipes that we have served over the years. Let the beer flow. Prost!

OKTOBERFEST MENU

APPETIZERS
Pan-Fried Potato Pancake with Apple Butter and Sour Cream
Bavarian Beer Potato Soup

MAIN COURSES
Wurst Platter of Bratwurst, Knackwurst, Weisswurst, Red Cabbage, Potato Salad, and Grainy Mustard
Jager-Schnitzel with Spätzle
Choucroute Garni

DESSERT
Linzer Torte
Fried Doughnut with Aventinus Pastry Cream

FEATURED BEERS

PAULANER OKTOBERFEST MÄRZEN
Made by: Paulaner Brauerei GmbH and Co
Style: Märzen
From: Germany
5.8% ABV
Serve in a stein

    This is a chestnut brown color. The flavor is toasted bread with a molasses malt balance and a subtle hop backbone. Pairs well with sausage, pretzels, and mustard.

PAULANER SALVATOR
Made by: Paulaner Brauerei GmbH and Co
Style: Dopplebock
From: Germany
7.9% ABV
Serve in a dimple glass

    This beer pours a hazy copper color. This is the first beer brewed by Paulaner. This beer is sweet and malty with dark fruit flavors, little hops. Very warming.

PAULANER OKTOBERFEST BIER
Made by: Paulaner Brauerei GmbH and Co
Style: Wiesn
From: Germany
6% ABV
Serve in a stein

    This is a golden color. This beer is poured in the tents in Munich. It is a balanced lager with malty sweetness and subtle hops. This beer pairs well with Jager Schnitzel, sausage, and pretzels.

JEVER PILSENER
Made by: Friesisches Brauhaus Zu Jever GmbH and Co
Style: pilsner
From: Germany
4.9% ABV
Serve in a pilsner glass

    This beer pours a clear straw color with a big, dense, white head. The flavor is clean, clear and dry, bready malt and bitter hop finish. This beer pairs well with fried foods, sandwiches, and burgers.

ERDINGER WEISSBIER KRISTALLKLAR
Made by: Erdinger Weissbräu
Style: Kristalweizen
From: Germany
5.3% ABV
Serve in a weizen glass

This beer pours crystal clear gold, it is extremely carbonated. The flavor has notes of orange, clove, caramel, and wet grass. This beer pairs well with salad, sandwiches, and fried foods.

SCHNEIDER WEISSE TAP 6 UNSER AVENTINUS
Made by: Weisses Bräuhaus G Schneider and Sohn GmbH
Style: Weizenbock
From: Germany
8.2% ABV
Serve in a weizen glass

This beer pours dark ruby-brown with an off white head. This beer taste of dark fruits, spice, and rich, nutty malt sweetness. This beer is made for chocolate desserts, barbeque sauces, and stews.

WEIHENSTEPHANER HEFEWEISSBIER
Made by: Bayerische Staatsbrauerei Weihenstephan
Style: Hefeweizen
From: Germany
5.4% ABV
Serve in a weizen glass

This beer pours a cloudy golden color with thick white head. The taste is spicy clove, bready yeast, strong banana notes with a grassy hop finish. This beer pairs with salad, light desserts, and seafood.

RECIPES

APPLE BUTTER

This is a creamy, apple puree that can be served alone, with cheese or in this case paired with the potato pancake.

Makes 3 cups

5 medium apples, peeled and seeded

4 ounces unsalted butter

1 teaspoon cinnamon

$\frac{1}{2}$ teaspoon nutmeg

$\frac{1}{4}$ teaspoon cloves

Peel and core the apples. Cut them into medium-sized pieces. In a saucepan, melt the butter and add the apples and spices. Cook the apples over medium heat, covered for about 20 minutes or until the apples become soft. When the apples are soft, add them to a blender and puree until the apples are smooth. Cool the apple butter and serve.

GERMAN POTATO PANCAKES

This is a great Oktoberfest appetizer paired with a nice pilsner. These potato pancakes are crunchy and are complemented beautifully by apple butter and sour cream.

Makes 8 pancakes

2 eggs

2 tablespoons all-purpose flour

$^1/_4$ teaspoon baking powder

10 sprigs parsley, leaves only

1 cup milk

$^1/_2$ teaspoon salt

$^1/_4$ teaspoon pepper

6 medium potatoes, peeled and shredded

$^1/_2$ cup finely chopped onion

$^1/_4$ cup vegetable oil

In a large bowl mix together the eggs, flour, baking powder, salt, pepper, potatoes, and onions.

Heat oil in a large skillet over medium heat. In batches, drop heaping spoonfuls of the potato mixture into the skillet. Press to flatten. Cook about 3 minutes on each side, until browned and crisp. Drain on paper. Serve with sour cream and apple butter.

BAVARIAN BEER POTATO SOUP

This is a traditional German potato soup. It is full of flavor and pairs perfectly with your favorite German beer.

Makes about 10 cups of soup

$^1/_2$ pound hickory-smoked bacon, medium dice

1 large stalk celery, medium dice

1 large white onion, medium dice

$^1/_2$ bunch parsley, chopped

$^1/_4$ teaspoon marjoram

$1^1/_2$ pounds red bliss potatoes, peeled and diced

$^1/_4$ cup all-purpose flour

6 cups beef broth

$^1/_4$ cup beer

Salt and pepper to taste

1 cup crème fraiche

3 tablespoons fresh chives, chopped

Render bacon in a stockpot over low heat until the fat melts out and the meat begins to get crunchy. Add the celery, onions, parsley, and marjoram.

Sauté ingredients until they are transparent. Stir in the potatoes and flour, being sure to coat vegetables evenly with the flour. Incorporate the beef broth and simmer for 30 to 40 minutes stirring occasionally. Season to taste with salt and pepper. Garnish the soup with crème fraiche and fresh chives.

WURST PLATTER

Sausage, sausage, and more sausage. We cook ours in beer and serve them with red cabbage and German potato salad.

Serves 6–8 people
750 ml Märzen beer
1 pound Knockwurst sausage
1 pound Bratwurst sausage
1 pound Weissewurst sausage

Put the sausage and beer in a large pot. Cook over medium heat to 160 degrees for about 10–15 minutes or until the sausage is warm all the way through. Be careful not to boil the sausages; they will split open if they get too hot.

RED CABBAGE

This cabbage is just the right combination of savory and sweet. It complements bratwurst perfectly.

Makes 6 servings
1 medium head red cabbage
1/4 cup brown sugar
1/4 cup apple cider vinegar
1 teaspoon salt
1 teaspoon pepper

2 medium onions
2 bay leaves
2 whole cloves
4 medium sized tart apple, julienned

Remove and discard wilted outer leaves of cabbage. Rinse cabbage and cut into quarters. Discard core. Coarsely shred cabbage.

Combine all ingredients in a large pot and bring to a simmer for half an hour over medium heat. Cover the pan halfway and continue cooking for another half an hour or until cabbage is tender. Cool and store for up to a week.

GERMAN POTATO SALAD

This potato salad is a refreshing option for picnics or for those who prefer a non-mayonnaise-based potato salad.

Makes 4 cups
1 pound red skin potatoes, boiled and skin on
1/4 cup white onions, small dice
1/4 cup celery, small dice
2 tablespoons fresh parsley, chopped
1/4 tablespoon olive oil
1 tablespoon cider vinegar
1 tablespoon beer

1 tablespoon whole grain mustard
1 teaspoon caraway seed
Salt and pepper to taste

Cover potatoes with water in saucepan. Bring to boil, then reduce heat and simmer uncovered until potatoes are fork tender, about 20 minutes. Drain the potatoes and cut potatoes into bite-sized pieces.

Combine in large bowl with onions, celery, and parsley.

In another bowl, whisk together oil, vinegar, beer, mustard, caraway seeds, salt, and pepper. Pour dressing over warm potato mix and gently toss. Salad is best when served warm or room temperature.

JÄGER SCHNITZEL

Schnitzel is a traditional German dish. We have added a creamy mushroom sauce that complements the crunchy breaded pork and the egg spätzle perfectly. We love to drink a big, cold mug of marzen with this dish.

Serves 4 people
For the Schnitzel
1 pound thin pork cutlets
$1/2$ teaspoon salt
$1/8$ teaspoon freshly ground pepper
$1/3$ cup all-purpose flour
2 eggs, lightly beaten
1 cup bread crumbs, fine
1 cup vegetable oil

For the Sauce
1 pound button mushrooms,
washed and cut into bite-size slices
2 teaspoons tomato paste
3 slices bacon, finely chopped
1 small white onion, finely chopped
$1/2$ cup chicken broth
$1/2$ cup cream
1 tablespoon sour cream
4 stems of fresh thyme
4 stems parsley
Salt and fresh pepper, to taste
2 tablespoons butter

Begin with the sauce first. Place chopped bacon in cold saute pan and render over low heat until fat begins to melt. Add the onions, and cook until they become soft and the bacon starts to become crunchy. Remove from pan and set aside in a separate bowl.

Melt butter in the pan the bacon and onions were cooked in, and add the sliced mushrooms. Cook over medium heat until mushrooms begin to soften; this takes about 4 minutes. Add the bacon mixture and tomato paste to the mushrooms. Stir together and add the chicken broth and thyme. Cook over medium heat until reduced to a quarter of the original volume. Remove the thyme when finished reducing.

Stir in cream, sour cream, salt, pepper, and the parsley. Continue cooking over low heat until combined. Remove from heat and set aside in a warm area.

Make the schnitzel. Pound the pork cutlets into $1/8$ inch thick slices. The best way of doing this is to lay out a large piece of plastic wrap on the counter or a large cutting board. Place the pork one piece at a time on the plastic and cover with another large piece of plastic wrap. Pound with a meat tenderizer. Remove the pork cutlet from plastic and set aside.

Mix the flour with the salt and pepper. Place the flour mix, eggs, and bread crumbs in three separate medium sized bowls. Arrange the bowls in a row. Bread each piece of pork by coating the pork in the flour mix, then dipping into the eggs, and finishing with a coat of bread crumbs. Set aside until ready to cook. (These can be prepared an hour in advance and held in the refrigerator.)

Heat the oil in a large, heavy skillet or pan over high heat until it reaches 350 degrees. Carefully place the breaded pork cutlet into the hot pan. Cook on each side for about 3 minutes, or until each side is a deep golden brown. Remove from the heat and serve with the schnitzel sauce and spätzle.

EGG SPÄTZLE

This dish is paired with the pork schnitzel and an amazing creamy mushroom sauce.

Serves 4 people
1¹/₄ cups all-purpose flour
¹/₂ teaspoon salt
1 extra large egg
6 tablespoons milk
3 tablespoons unsalted butter, melted
1 tablespoon fresh parsley, chopped

Combine flour and salt in a bowl. Make a well in the center. Whisk the egg and the milk together, and pour it into the well of the dry ingredients. Mix the ingredients with a wooden spoon, until the batter is elastic. You can also combine these ingredients in a tabletop mixer with the paddle attachment on medium heat, being careful not to over mix.

Push the spätzle dough through a spätzle maker (or a colander can be used. Pour the mix into the colander over boiling water, salted water and press it through with the wooden spoon).

Cook uncovered for about 8 minutes. Drain spätzle. Spätzle can be cooled and stored for up to 3 days or served immediately. When ready to serve, combine the melted butter with parsley, salt, and pepper in a large pan, and add the spätzle. Warm for 4–5 minutes over medium heat.

CHOUCROUTE GARNI

This is a seriously meaty one pot dish.

Serves 6–8 people
4 ounces unsalted butter
8 pieces bacon, thick cut and chopped
1 white onion, medium dice
1 shallot, medium dice
2 cloves garlic, minced
3 carrots, medium dice
12 small red bliss potatoes
3 bay leaves
12 sprigs parsley
4 sprigs thyme
4 cups chicken stock
750 ml Märzen beer
$\frac{1}{2}$ tablespoon salt and pepper
3 pounds sauerkraut
1 pound Knockwurst sausage
1 pound Bratwurst sausage
1 pound Weissewurst sausage
6 4-ounce smoked pork chops
6 apples, sliced

In a large pot melt 3 ounces of butter and 6 pieces of chopped bacon. Render the bacon fat over medium heat. When bacon begins to brown, add the onions, shallots, and garlic. Cook until the onions become translucent and begin to caramelize. Add the carrots, potatoes, stock, beer, herbs, salt, pepper, sauerkraut, and simmer for 20 minutes. Add the sausage and pork chops, and cook for another 15 minutes. While the sausage is cooking, melt one ounce of butter and cook two pieces of bacon until they becomes crispy. Add the apples and sauté until they are soft, season to taste. When sausage is finished cooking, plate the ingredients in a large bowl.

Each serving should have a large spoonful of sauerkraut, one of each sausage, one pork chop, two potatoes, and carrot pieces. Spoon the apple-bacon garnish over top. Serve with grainy mustard and a Märzen beer.

LINZER TORTE

This is a traditional dish served around Christmas in Germany, but we love it so much that we enjoy it anytime we can. We have chosen to make our dough with almond flour, but it can be made with hazelnuts or walnuts.

Makes 1 12x2-inch torte

1$^1/_2$ cups almond flour
1$^1/_2$ cups all-purpose flour
$^1/_3$ cup sugar
1 lemon, zested
1 teaspoon cinnamon
$^1/_4$ teaspoon cloves
$^1/_2$ teaspoon baking powder
$^1/_4$ teaspoon kosher salt
$^1/_3$ pound unsalted butter, cut into small pieces
2 egg yolks
1 teaspoon vanilla
$^3/_4$ cup raspberry jam

Place the almond flour in a food processor and blend until the flour is a fine dust.

Combine the flours, sugar, lemon zest, spices, baking powder, and salt in a mixing bowl with the paddle attachment. Mix the ingredients and add the butter. Mix until the butter is in pea-sized pieces. Add the eggs and vanilla and mix until the ingredients become dough.

Wrap the dough and refrigerate for 1 hour. When the dough is cold, split it in half and roll half out on a floured surface. Mold it into a greased 12"x2" pan. Spread the raspberry jam into the crust. Roll the second half of the dough and cut it into strips, weaving the dough to create a top crust. Seal the edges of the torte by pinching the bottom and the top crust together. Bake at 350 degrees for about 45 minutes or until the dough becomes golden brown and the jam begins to bubble.

RASPBERRY JAM

It is easier to buy raspberry jam—but not one that features this delightful raspberry Lambic! This recipe is so flavorful, so fresh tasting. Use it on toast or in desserts.

Makes 3 cups

8 cups raspberries, fresh or frozen
2 cups sugar
1 orange, zested and juiced
$^1/_4$ cup raspberry Lambic
2 packages powdered fruit pectin
$^3/_4$ cup water

In a large bowl, combine the raspberries, sugar, Lambic, orange zest, and juice. Gently smash the fruit mixture and remove half the fruit and blend in the blender until smooth. In a small saucepan, combine the pectin and the water. Bring the water-pectin mix to a boil and boil for 1 minute. Be sure not to boil longer than 1 minute. Reduce the heat and add the fruit to the pectin and stir for 3 to 4 minutes. Remove the jam from the pot and put it in a bowl to chill, covered for at least 2 hours. Store in refrigerator for up to 2 weeks.

FRIED DOUGHNUTS

This is a really easy recipe to make. These doughnuts are best served right out of the fryer with pastry cream.

Makes 20–30 doughnuts
$^1/_2$ cup unsalted butter
1 cup water
1 tablespoon Bock beer
1 tablespoon sugar
$^1/_4$ teaspoon salt
1 cup all-purpose flour
4 eggs
6 cups vegetable oil
$^1/_3$ cup powdered sugar

Combine the butter, water, beer, salt, and sugar in a medium pot. Bring these ingredients to a boil and stir in the flour with a wooden spoon. Stir until the mix becomes dough and pulls away from the edges of the pot. Place the dough into a mixer with a paddle attachment, begin mixing the dough on medium heat, and add one egg at a time until all the eggs are incorporated.

Heat the oil in a thick-bottomed medium-sized pan to 340 degrees. When the oil reaches the desired temperature, drop 1 tablespoon at a time of the dough into the oil. Fry for about 3 minutes, turning once to brown both sides of the doughnut. The center will come out clean when stuck with a toothpick. Serve hot.

AVENTINUS PASTRY CREAM

This cream can be used for a cake filling or sauce for desserts. The Aventinus gives this cream a caramel, fruity twist. This is a favorite dish served with fresh fried doughnuts.

Makes 2$^1/_2$ cups
2 cups whole milk
$^1/_4$ cup Aventinus beer
1 teaspoon vanilla
$^2/_3$ cup sugar
$^1/_4$ cup cornstarch
4 egg yolks
2 tablespoons unsalted butter

Fill a large bowl with ice and a medium bowl to place on top of the ice. Combine the milk, beer, and vanilla in a medium pot. Bring the milk to a simmer. Combine the sugar and cornstarch in a medium bowl, whisk in the egg yolks. Slowly temper the hot milk mix into the egg-starch mix. Return the mix to the pot and heat over medium

heat. Whisk constantly until the mix begins to bubble. Boil for 1 minute to be sure the starch is cooked out. When the custard has boiled, quickly pour the custard into the medium bowl on the ice. Stir the custard to cool. it down. Add the butter and stir until all combined. Let the custard cool completely and serve or store in the refrigerator.

THANKSGIVING

Family get-togethers have certainly changed a lot since my siblings and I were kids; our palates are more sophisticated and our gatherings have become joyous and fun. For our family, nothing fits the bill better than a fantastic assortment of incredible beers to match with our traditional Thanksgiving meal. Challenge each of your guests to bring a fantastic bottle of beer to share. For us, beer is the new wine!

THANKSGIVING MENU
Beer Smoked Turkey with gravy
Garlicky Kale Salad with dried cherries and toasted almonds
Baked Macaroni and Cheese
Butternut Squash Stuffing
Mushroom and Wild Rice Dressing

Cranberry Beer Sauce
Apple Cider Pie
Dubbel Pumpkin Pie
Banana Cream Pie
Chocolate Cream Pie

FEATURED BEERS

LANSDOWNE

Made by: Crispin Cider Company
Style: Hard Cider
From: California
6.9% ABV
Serve in a lager glass

This beer pours a hazy rich brown color. This beer is made with Irish stout yeast and taste like unfiltered apple cider with hints of butterscotch, molasses, and fruitiness with a buttery mouthfeel. This beer pairs well with apple desserts, cheese, and stewed and roasted meats.

SOFIE

Made by: Goose Island Beer Company
Style: farmhouse ale
From: Illinois
6.5% ABV
Serve in a tulip glass

This beer pours a hazy straw color with a frothy white head. It has a strong white wine flavor with zested citrus and some malty sweetness. This beer pairs with roasted poultry, cheese, and spicy food.

LOCAL 1

Made by: Brooklyn Brewery
Style: Belgian Strong Ale
From: New York
9% ABV
Serve in an Trappist glass

This beer pours golden and tastes of sweet apple and pear with vanilla, bready sweetness, and a slight hop finish. This beer pairs well with salads, vegetables, fish, and chicken.

SAHTEA TRADITIONAL ALE
Made by: Dogfish Head Brewery
Style: sahti
From: Delaware
9% ABV
Serve in an English pint
    This beer pours pale golden amber in color. This beer is full of sweet malts with black tea, cardamom, cinnamon, ginger, cloves, black pepper, and juniper. This beer pairs with sweet potatoes and winter squash, apple and pears, and bread.

NUT BROWN ALE
Made by: Samuel Smith's Brewery
Style: English brown ale
From: England
5% ABV
Serve in an English pint glass
    This beer pours mahogany brown with a malty and sweet flavor. This beer is full of roasted nuts, some fruity and bready flavors balanced out with a light hops. This beer pairs well with cheese, smoked meats, steak, and charcuterie.

ABBEY ALE
Made by: Brewery Ommegang
Style: Dubbel
From: New York
8.5% ABV
Serve in a Trappist glass
    This beer pours a rich burgundy-amber color and a thick off white head. This beer tastes of dark fruit layered with caramel sugar and some honey balanced with a lightly charred malt and spicy, dry finish. This beer pairs with lamb, pork, slow cooked stews, barbecue, and rich cheese.

RYE BARREL AGED SMOKING WOOD
Made by: The Bruery
Style: Imperial smoked porter
From: California
10–13% ABV
Serve in a dimpled mug or lager glass

This beer is brewed with Beachwood and cherry wood smoked malt, and aged in rye whiskey barrels. It pours dark brown and smells like liquid barbeque. This intense beer taste of toasted oak, caramel, and vanilla which balances the smoke flavors. This beer pairs perfectly with smoked and roasted meats.

WELLS BANANA BREAD BEER
Made by: Wells and Young's Ltd
Style: English strong ale
From: England
5.2% ABV
Serve in a snifter

This beer pours copper in color and taste of ripe banana, bready malted sweetness, vanilla, and light hops. Pair this beer with sweet cream desserts and shortbread.

YOUNG'S DOUBLE CHOCOLATE STOUT

Made by: Well's and Young's Ltd
Style: Milk Stout
From: England
5.2% ABV
Serve in an English Pint

This beer pours dark brown with a thick mocha head. It tastes of roasted oats, dark bitter chocolate, and hints of espresso with a light lactic sweetness and a bitter finish. This beer pairs perfectly with dark chocolate and cream.

HUNAHPU'S IMPERIAL STOUT

Made by: Cigar City Brewing
Style: Imperial stout
From: Florida
11% ABV
Serve in a snifter

This beer pours jet black with a dark beige head. The flavor is of dark fruit, chocolate, vanilla, cinnamon and a touch of coffee bitterness with a chili spice finish. This beer pairs well with smoked meats, stews and dessert.

RECIPES

BEER SMOKED TURKEY WITH GRAVY

We started smoking our Thanksgiving turkey a few years ago and I don't think we will ever stop. The slow smoking and beer brine really creates a juicy, flavorful turkey.

Serves 6–8 people

1 15-pound whole turkey

1$\frac{1}{2}$ gallons Nut Brown Ale, enough to cover turkey completely

2 cups kosher salt

$\frac{1}{2}$ cup unsalted butter

$\frac{1}{2}$ cup all-purpose flour

8 cups chicken or turkey stock

$\frac{1}{4}$ cup Nut Brown Ale

Salt and pepper to taste

Marinate the turkey in 1$\frac{1}{2}$ gallons of beer with the salt for 24–48 hours in the refrigerator. (This step is optional, but absolutely worth the extra effort. The beer will not only infuse extra flavor into the meat but will also help tenderize it).

After the turkey has marinated, remove it from the beer and discard the beer used for marinating. Place it in a smoker at 190 degrees. (Put a large oven safe pan underneath the turkey to catch all of the drippings). Cook the turkey for 8–10 hours or until it is cooked through, about 170 degrees in the turkey breast. We prefer to smoke with oak wood, but other smoking woods that we recommend are hickory, applewood, and mesquite.

When the turkey is done, set it aside and finish the gravy. Bring the stock to a boil and set aside. Heat the butter and flour in a medium sauce pot over medium heat, stir with a wooden spoon. Be sure to scrape the bottom of the pan, stirring constantly. Keep stirring until the roux is peanut butter brown. When the roux is ready, slowly add the stock, one cup at a time until all the stock is incorporated. Add the pan drippings and simmer the gravy for 35–40 minutes. Add the $\frac{1}{4}$ cup fresh nut brown ale beer to your sauce and season with salt and pepper. Serve warm with the turkey.

GARLICKY KALE SALAD WITH DRIED CHERRIES AND TOASTED ALMONDS

This is a healthy addition to the Thanksgiving table and also a satisfying one. Try this salad anytime for a healthy lunch or dinner a well.

Serves 6 people

2 bunches kale, cut into bite-sized pieces

$1/4$ cup dried cherries

$1/4$ cup almonds, toasted and sliced

$1/2$ cup roasted garlic dressing

Toast the almonds in a 350 degree oven for about 5 minutes or until they are golden brown. Remove from the oven and cool. Combine the chopped kale, dried cherries, and almonds in a salad bowl. Toss with the roasted garlic dressing and serve.

ROASTED GARLIC SALAD DRESSING

This is a creamy dressing that can be used on any salad or use as a light pasta sauce.

Makes about 1 $^3/_4$ cups
2 heads garlic
2 teaspoons olive oil
1 cup sour cream
$^1/_2$ cup buttermilk
1 lemon, zested
$^1/_4$ cup farmhouse ale
$^1/_2$ teaspoon sea salt
$^1/_2$ teaspoon ground pepper

Coat the garlic heads with oil and wrap them each in foil, place them on a baking sheet and bake in a 350 degree oven for about 1 hour or until the garlic is tender. Let cool. When garlic is cool enough to handle squeeze the garlic out of the shells and put the garlic in a blender. Combine the sour cream, buttermilk, lemon zest, beer, salt, and pepper in the blender with the roasted garlic. Blend these ingredients until they are all combined and smooth. This dressing can be stored in the refrigerator for about 1 week.

BAKED MACARONI AND CHEESE

This is a creamy and delicious macaroni and cheese. This recipe can be made and served straight out of the pan or baked into a dish for a family-style side dish.

Serves 8–10 people

1 pound penne pasta

1 gallon water

2 tablespoons kosher salt

2 tablespoons olive oil

2 tablespoons unsalted butter

2 tablespoons all-purpose flour

2 cups whole milk

$1/4$ cup strong ale beer

$1/4$ cup white onion, small dice

4 black peppercorns

1 bay leaf

3 fresh parsley stalks

$1/8$ teaspoon nutmeg

1 teaspoon sea salt

$1/2$ teaspoon pepper

16 ounces parmesan cheese, fresh grated

16 ounces sharp cheddar cheese, grated

8 ounces Havarti cheese, grated

2 cups panko bread crumbs

Bring the water and salt to boil in a large stock pot. Add the pasta and stir. Bring the pasta back to a boil and simmer until it is tender, but firm to the bite. Drain the pasta in a colander, run cold over pasta until it is cool, and toss with the oil to prevent sticking. Set aside.

Put the milk and beer in a saucepan with the onion, peppercorns, bay leaf, parsley, and nutmeg. Bring to a boil and then turn off the heat. Allow to infuse for 15 minutes and then strain.

Melt the butter in a saucepan. Stir in the flour and cook for 1–2 minutes. Reduce the heat to low and gradually stir in the milk until it is all incorporated. Return the heat to medium-high to continue cooking the sauce, be sure to stir all the time, bring it to a boil. Simmer gently for 8–10 minutes and season with salt and pepper.

In a sauté pan, heat the sauce and add the 3 cheeses. Mix until they are melted and all incorporated. Stir in the pasta until it is hot and coated. Pour it into a baking dish and evenly coat it with the bread crumbs. Bake in a 350 degree oven for about 30 minutes or until it becomes bubbling and the bread crumbs are golden brown.

BUTTERNUT SQUASH STUFFING

This is a wonderful autumn stuffing. The combination of sage and creamy roasted squash really complements the Thanksgiving turkey.

Serves 8 people

1 butternut squash, medium dice

3 tablespoons olive oil

$^1/_4$ cup unsalted butter

1 yellow onion, medium dice

4 celery stalks, medium dice

2 tablespoons fresh sage

2 pounds white bread, cubed and dried

4 whole eggs

3$^1/_2$ cups vegetable stock

$^1/_4$ cup amber beer

1 teaspoon sea salt

$^1/_2$ teaspoon ground black pepper

Preheat the oven to 350 degrees. Peel, remove seeds and cut the squash and toss it in the olive oil and sprinkle it with salt and pepper. Spread the squash on a baking sheet and bake for about 1 hour or until the squash is tender. Set aside. While the squash is baking, cut the crust off the bread and cube the loaves. Spread the bread evenly on a baking sheet and toast until it becomes light brown. Remove from the oven and cool completely. In a large sauté pan melt the butter and sauté the onions for 3 minutes and then add the celery. Sauté the vegetables until the celery is tender. Add the sage, salt, and pepper, sauté for 1 minute. Remove the vegetables and combine them with the squash and bread cubes in a large bowl. In a separate bowl whisk together the vegetable broth, beer, and the eggs. Pour the broth mix over the bread mix. Gently fold all the ingredients together. Pour the stuffing mix into a greased baking dish. Bake the stuffing for 35–40 minutes or until the stuffing becomes golden brown and starts to puff up. Serve hot.

CRANBERRY SAUCE

When I was a kid I loved canned cranberry sauce, and would insist that it be left in the can shape so I could slice it into circles. Those days are long gone and now I cannot imagine our holiday table without Luther's fresh cranberry sauce.

Serves 10–12 people

12 ounces fresh cranberries
$^1/_2$ cup farmhouse ale
$^1/_2$ cup pineapple juice
1 cup sugar
1 lime, zested

In a medium saucepan, combine the cranberries, beer, pineapple juice, sugar, and lime zest. Cook over medium-high heat for 15 minutes. The cranberries will become soft and burst, and the sauce will begin to reduce slightly. The sauce will thicken as it cools.

WILD RICE AND MUSHROOM DRESSING

This is a dish my mom used to make when I was a child. We enjoy it during the holidays, but it also makes a great side dish for dinner any night.

Makes 8–10 servings

1 medium yellow onion, small dice

3 garlic cloves, crushed

1 tablespoon olive oil

4 celery stalks, small dice

1½ cups fresh mushrooms, cremini, portabella, and oyster

3 cups vegetable stock

¼ cup amber beer

2 cups cream of mushroom soup

6 ounces wild rice

4 ounces long grain rice

Preheat the oven to 350 degrees. In a hot dutch oven add the olive oil, onions, and garlic, sauté the onions and garlic until they become translucent, add the celery and sauté for about 5 minutes. Add the mushrooms and gently sauté for 3 minutes more. Mix into the vegetables the stock, beer, and mushroom soup. Stir in the uncooked rice and cover the pot. Place the rice mix in the oven and cook for about 1 hour or until the rice is fully cooked.

THREE MUSHROOM SOUP

This soup is great on its own for lunch or it can be incorporated into other dishes like wild rice dressing or green bean casserole.

Serves 6 people

2 cups cremini mushrooms
2 cups portabella mushrooms
2 cups oyster mushrooms
1 cup white onions, small dice
1 teaspoon fresh thyme
1¹/₂ cups vegetable stock
3 tablespoons unsalted butter
3 tablespoons all-purpose flour
¹/₄ teaspoon sea salt
¹/₄ teaspoon black pepper
1 cup half and half
2 tablespoons amber beer

In a large pot combine the mushrooms, onions, thyme, and vegetable stock and cook for 10–15. Place the mushroom mix in a blender and pulse to create a chunky puree. In a same pot the mushrooms were cooked in, add the butter and melt it, whisking the flour and butter together with the salt and pepper. Add the half and half, beer, and mushroom puree. Bring to a boil and cook until the soup becomes thick.

APPLE CIDER PIE

Many years of making apple pie have led to this recipe. The combination of hard apple cider and fresh cooked apples really sets this pie apart.

Makes 1 9-inch pie

2 9-inch pie shells, top and bottom shells

6 apples, peeled, cored, and sliced

¹/₄ cup unsalted butter

1 cup brown sugar

1 teaspoon cinnamon

¹/₂ teaspoon nutmeg

¹/₄ teaspoon ginger

¹/₄ teaspoon cloves

1 teaspoon vanilla

1 cup hard apple cider

2 tablespoons cornstarch

1 tablespoon water

Peel, core, and slice your apples; ¹/₄ inch thick slices work well. In a large sauté pan melt your butter and then stir in the brown sugar, spices, and vanilla. Cook this butter mix on high heat until the sugar is dissolved and bubbling. Pour the sliced apples into the butter mix and stir to coat all the apples, pour the cider over the apples and cover the pan. Cook the apples for about 10 minutes or until they become soft but not mushy, stir occasionally. When the apples are cooked, strain them from the liquid in the pan, being sure to save the cooking liquid from the apples.

Set the cooked apples aside in a bowl and return the apple juice from cooking to the pan. Bring the juice to a boil, while the mix is heating up combine the cornstarch and water until the starch is liquefied. When the apple juice has reached a full boil quickly whisk the cornstarch slurry into the apple juice. The mix will thicken quickly and continue to boil. Cook for 1 minute and remove from the heat. Pour the thickened apple juice into the cooked apples and mix together. Pour the apples into the prepared pie crust and cover it with the second crust to create a closed pie. Make a few small holes in the top crust for the pie to vent. Brush the top of the pie with an egg wash and sprinkle it with sugar. Bake in the oven at 350 degrees of about 45 minutes or until the crust is golden brown and the filling is bubbling. Serve warm with ice cream.

DUBBEL PUMPKIN PIE

Pumpkin pie is a traditional dessert served during the holidays. We have taken the basic pumpkin pie and turned it up a bit by adding a rich dubbel abbey ale. This pie still satisfies the traditional palates, but just brings a little more flavor and complexity to a basic dessert.

Makes 1 9-inch pie

1 9-inch pie shell
15 ounces pumpkin puree
14 ounces sweetened condensed milk
3 large eggs
1 teaspoon cinnamon
1 teaspoon nutmeg
$^1/_2$ teaspoon ginger
$^1/_2$ teaspoon allspice
1 teaspoon vanilla
3 tablespoon dubbel beer

Preheat the oven to 350 degrees. Combine all the ingredients into a large bowl and whisk until they are all combined and the mix is smooth. Pour the mix into the prepared pie shell. Bake the pie for about 45 minutes or until the pie is no longer wobbly when lightly shaken. Do not over cook the pie; the top should not be browned or cracked. Remove from the oven and chill.

BANANA CREAM PIE

In our house, cream pie beats out pumpkin as the favorite. We love, banana, coconut, and chocolate cream pie. For this pie, we have combined with Well's Banana Bread Beer, because it adds so much yummy malt flavor and bitter hops that balance out the sweet bananas and sugar in the pie.

Makes 1 9-inch pie
2$^1/_2$ cups graham cracker crumbs
$^1/_3$ cup sugar
$^1/_2$ cup unsalted butter, melted
1 tablespoon vanilla
1$^1/_2$ cups heavy whipping cream
1$^1/_2$ cups whole milk
$^1/_2$ cup sugar
$^1/_2$ cup cornstarch
$^1/_4$ teaspoon sea salt
4 large egg yolks
1 teaspoon vanilla
$^1/_4$ cup banana beer
2 tablespoons unsalted butter
5 ripe bananas, peeled, cut into slices

For the crust, preheat oven to 350 degrees. Stir the graham cracker crumbs, sugar, vanilla, and butter until all combined. Press the mix into a 9-inch pie dish. Chill until firm, about 30 minutes. Bake crust until set, about 15 minutes. Cool completely.

For the filling, combine the heavy cream and milk in medium saucepan. Bring mix to simmer. Combine the sugar, cornstarch, and salt in medium bowl. When the milk mix comes to a simmer, remove from the heat. Add the egg yolks, beer, and vanilla to the sugar-starch mix and whisk until smooth. Slowly temper the milk mix into the sugar and egg mix until all combined. Pour the entire mix back into the pot and bring to a boil for about 1 minute. Continue stirring the custard the whole time. When the custard is thick and bubbling remove from heat quickly and pour it into another bowl to cool off quickly. (I recommend a large bowl full of ice with a slightly small bowl sitting on top of the ice). Add the butter to the custard and mix until all combined. Let the custard cool completely.

To assemble the pie, line the crust with a layer of bananas, layer half the custard over bananas, and then layer more bananas on the custard, next layer the rest of the custard on the bananas. Let the pie set at least 1 hour, Serve with whipped cream.

CHOCOLATE CREAM PIE

My father's favorite Thanksgiving dessert. Here is our twist on this classic pie.

Makes 1 9-inch pie

2¹/₂ cups dry chocolate cookies crumbs

¹/₃ cup sugar

¹/₂ cup unsalted butter, melted

1 tablespoon vanilla

1¹/₂ cups heavy whipping cream

1¹/₂ cups whole milk

³/₄ cup sugar

¹/₃ cup cornstarch

¹/₂ cup cocoa powder

¹/₄ teaspoon sea salt

4 large egg yolks

1 teaspoon vanilla

¹/₄ cup chocolate stout

¹/₂ cup dark chocolate chips

2 tablespoons unsalted butter

For the crust, preheat oven to 350 degrees. Stir the graham cracker crumbs, sugar, vanilla, and butter until all combined. Press the mix into a 9-inch pie dish. Chill until firm, about 30 minutes. Bake crust until set, about 15 minutes. Cool completely.

For the filling, combine the heavy cream and milk in medium saucepan. Bring mix to simmer. Combine the sugar, cornstarch, cocoa, and salt in medium bowl. When the milk mix comes to a simmer, remove from the heat. Add the egg yolks, beer, and vanilla to the sugar-starch mix and whisk until smooth. Slowly temper the milk mix into the sugar and egg mix until all combined. Pour the entire mix back into the pot and bring to a boil for about one minute. Continue stirring the custard the whole time. When the custard is thick and bubbling, remove from heat quickly and pour into another bowl to cool off quickly. (I recommend a large bowl full of ice with a slightly small bowl sitting on top of the ice.) Whisk the chocolate pieces into the custard; mix until the chocolate is completely melted. Add the butter to the custard and mix until all combined. Let the custard cool completely.

To assemble the pie, pour the filling into the chocolate shell and let the pie set at least 1 hour in the refrigerator. Serve with whipped cream.

GASTROPUB CLASSICS

Gas·tro·pub\gas-trō-pub\ n: a relaxed setting for enjoying excellent food along with draught beers and wines from around the world.

Over the years, we have made a lot of food at The Horse and Hound Gastropub. We have experimented a lot with different flavors and pairings. This chapter features some of the dishes that our loyal clientele are especially partial to, from the poached pear salad and creamy shrimp and grits to the dreamy homemade beer marshmallows. We dedicate this chapter to all the wonderful people who have supported our restaurant over the years. We hope you enjoy these recipes as much as our regulars have.

GASTROPUB FAVORITES MENU
1st Course
> Ginger Poached Pear Salad with spring greens, candied pecans, crumbled blue cheese, Ginger vinaigrette
>
> Crabbie's Alcoholic Ginger Beer, Halewood International LTD, England

2nd Course
> Shrimp and Grits with creamy corn grits, shrimp, sautéed vegetables, country ham, veal Imperial Bock demi-glace
>
> Samuel Smith's Yorkshire Stingo, Samuel Smith Brewery, England

3rd Course
> Dark Ale Marshmallow Dream with flourless stout cake, peanut butter mousse and peanuts
>
> Brother Thelonious Strong Dark Ale, North Coast Brewery, California

FEATURED BEERS

CRABBIE'S ALCOHOLIC GINGER BEER

Made by: Halewood International Ltd
Style: Ginger beer
From: England
4.0% ABV
Serve in a tumbler glass

This beer pours clear golden amber in color and tastes of strong ginger spice. It is sweet, spicy, and easy to drink. This beer pairs well with salad and desserts.

YORKSHIRE STINGO

Made by: Samuel Smith Old Brewery
Style: English strong ale
From: England
9% ABV
Serve in an English pint

This beer pours a hazy orange-amber color. This is a very complex beer tasting of sweet malts, graham crackers, dark fruit, some oakiness and earthy hops. This beer pairs well with ham, cream, roasted meats, steak, and dessert.

BROTHER THELONIOUS

Made by: North Coast Brewery
Style: Strong Dark Ale
From: California
9.4% ABV
Serve in a Trappist glass

This beer pours a dark walnut brown. This beer is bready, very sweet and malty with some cherry, fig, and nutty undertones. This beer pairs with creamy cheese and desserts.

RECIPES

GINGER POACHED PEAR SALAD

This salad has been on our menu at The Horse and Hound Gastropub since we opened. It is a staple for us and a favorite for our customers. The poached pears and blue cheese complement one another beautifully.

Serves 6 people

3 pears, peeled, seeded and cut in half
3 cups ginger beer
$1/2$ cup sugar
1 cinnamon stick
3 whole cloves
$1/2$ cup sugar
$1/4$ cup water
$1^1/2$ cups pecan halves
1 tablespoon unsalted butter
pinch salt
6 cups mixed spring greens
3 ounces blue cheese

Pour the beer in a medium pot with $1/2$ cup of sugar, cinnamon stick, and whole cloves, stir and bring the mix to a simmer. Add the pears to the simmering liquid, simmer for about 15 minutes or until they are tender but not mushy. (Keep an eye on the pears because cooking time will vary depending on the ripeness and size of your pears). When the pears are tender, remove them from the heat and set aside. For best results, make the pears the day before and refrigerate overnight in the poaching liquid.

In a medium saucepan, combine $1/2$ cup of sugar and $1/2$ cup of water, mix the two together and use a little bit of water to brush the sides of the pan clean. Bring the sugar to a simmer over high heat; cook the sugar until it becomes a light amber color. When the sugar is the right color, add the butter and pinch of salt, mix the butter with a wooden spoon and then add the pecans, stir until the nuts are coated, pour the candied nuts onto a greased pan and let cool. When the candied pecans are cooled, chop them into bite-sized pieces and set aside.

To assemble the salad, place the greens in the bowl and dress with the vinaigrette. Sprinkle the blue cheese and nuts evenly on the salad. Slice the poached pears and add them to the salad. Enjoy.

GINGER VINAIGRETTE

This dressing is a little spicy and is perfect for salads or marinating meat.

....

Makes 1¹/₂ cups

1 cup extra virgin olive oil
¹/₂ cup Ginger beer
¹/₄ cup sugar
3 tablespoons fresh ginger root, peeled and grated
1 clove garlic, minces
1 teaspoon sea salt
¹/₂ teaspoon fresh ground pepper

Combine all ingredients in a blender except the oil. Blend the ingredients until completely combined and chopped up. Add the oil in a steady stream until all incorporated. Serve on salad. May be stored for up to 1 week.

SHRIMP AND GRITS

A southern tradition that we serve at brunch as well as dinner. This recipe is our Gastropub's best seller. The combination of creamy corn grits, jumbo shrimp, sautéed vegetables, and veal demi-glace is a serious winner.

Serves 6 people

30 large shrimp, peeled and deveined

1¹/₂ cups white onions, small dice

³/₄ cup carrots, small dice

³/₄ cup celery, small dice

³/₄ cup country ham, small dice

³/₄ cup demi-glace

1 cup heavy cream

6 tablespoons strong ale

6 cups grits

In a hot sauté pan, add country ham and sauté until it becomes crisp, add diced vegetables and sauté for 2 minutes. Add the shrimp to the pan and cook for 2 minutes, then add the demi-glace and cook for 2 minutes. Add the cream and simmer for 2 minutes, then add the beer, simmer for 1 minute more. Pour the sauce and shrimp over the grits. Serve hot.

See recipe for grits, page 194.

See recipe for veal demi-glace, page 56.

MARSHMALLOW DREAM

This is a show stopper. The creamy peanut butter mousse really balances out the sweet, soft marshmallows and complements the flourless cake layer. Make these and slice into bars for a real treat.

Makes 1 9x9-inch pan

1 9x9-inch flourless stout cake

1 9x9-inch pan of dark ale marshmallows

4–6 cups peanut butter mousse

1 cup peanuts

Bake the chocolate flourless cake and refrigerate for 2–3 hours or until cool. Make the marshmallows and pour them over the chilled chocolate cake in the same pan. Let the marshmallows set-up overnight in the refrigerator. Make the peanut butter mousse and refrigerate overnight. When you are ready to serve the dessert, remove cake and marshmallow layers from the pan, pipe or spread the mousse on the top of the marshmallows. Sprinkle the peanuts on the top and cut into pieces. Serve.

FLOURLESS STOUT CAKE

This is a rich, decadent, and very moist cake. Serve it on its own or use it as a layer for our marshmallow dream.

Makes 1 9x9-inch pan
6 ounces dark chocolate, 60–70%
recommended
$^3/_4$ cup unsalted butter
$1^1/_4$ cups sugar
$^3/_4$ cup cocoa powder
5 whole eggs
1 teaspoon vanilla
4 tablespoons dark beer

In a double boiler, combine the chocolate and the butter, melt and set aside. In a medium size bowl, combine the sugar, cocoa powder, eggs, vanilla, and beer; whisk until all combined. Whisk in the warm chocolate mix and stir until all combined. Pour the mix into a greased pan and bake for 30 minutes in a 300 degree oven.

DARK ALE MARSHMALLOWS

These marshmallows can be made with almost any beer, but we recommend something malty.

Makes 18 marshmallows
2 egg whites, room temperature
2 cups sugar
1 tablespoon corn syrup
$1^1/_2$ cups water
4 tablespoons unflavored
powdered gelatin
1 teaspoon vanilla
4 tablespoons dark ale

In a mixing bowl, whisk the egg whites to soft peaks. In a small bowl combine $^1/_2$ cup ice cold water with the gelatin, let sit for 5 minutes. Then melt over medium heat, but do not boil. While the whites are whipping, combine the sugar, corn syrup, and $^3/_4$ cup of water in a small sauce pot; brush the sides of the pot with a wet pastry brush to clean. Cook the sugar until it reaches 250–265 degrees.

When the sugar is the right temperature, whisk the melted gelatin into the syrup. The syrup will then slowly be added to the egg whites while they whisk on a medium-slow speed. In a thin, slow stream along the inside edge of the bowl stream the syrup mix into the eggs until all combined. Whisk the mix until the marshmallows have cooled and reach firm peaks.

If serving on their own, pour the marshmallows into a greased pan and let them set-up overnight. Cut in pieces and coat with powdered sugar. If using for the marshmallow dream, pour the marshmallow over the chocolate cake.

PEANUT BUTTER MOUSSE

We love this mousse. It is delicate and creamy with just enough sweetness. It is great on its own or as a cake filling.

Makes about 8 cups

1 cup peanut butter

1/2 cup unsalted butter

2 teaspoons unflavored gelatin

4 tablespoons water

1/2 cup sugar

8 egg yolks

1 teaspoon vanilla

4 tablespoons dark beer

2 cups heavy whipping cream

In a double boiler, melt the peanut butter and the butter. While the peanut butter is melting, combine the gelatin powder with 3 tablespoons cold water, let it sit about 5 minutes.

In a mixing bowl add the egg yolks and whisk until they become light yellow and fluffy. While the yolks are being whisked combine the sugar and 1 tablespoon water in a small sauté pan. Cook the sugar until it begins to boil and then cook for 1 minute more, remove from heat and slowly pour into the egg yolk mix. (Turn the mixer down to low and pour the hot sugar in a constant but slow stream into the egg yolks. Be sure to pour along the inside edge of the bowl, keeping it out of the whisk).

When all the sugar is combined with the egg yolks, continue to mix until the yolks are cool and hold soft peaks. Place the set gelatin in a sauce pan and gently melt the gelatin, being sure to warm just until melted. Do not overcook. Once the gelatin is melted temper it into the egg yolk mix.

Combine the egg-gelatin mix with the warm, melted peanut butter, whisk together until smooth. Whisk the heavy cream, beer, and vanilla in a mixing bowl. Whisk until soft peaks form. Gently fold the cream mix into the peanut butter mix. Do not over mix, as it is important to keep the air in the mix. Refrigerate for at least 4 hours or until firm. Serve cold.

METRIC AND IMPERIAL CONVERSIONS

(These conversions are rounded for convenience)

Ingredient	Cups/Tablespoons/ Teaspoons	Ounces	Grams/Milliliters
Butter	1 cup=16 tablespoons= 2 sticks	8 ounces	230 grams
Cream cheese	1 tablespoon	0.5 ounce	14.5 grams
Cheese, shredded	1 cup	4 ounces	110 grams
Cornstarch	1 tablespoon	0.3 ounce	8 grams
Flour, all-purpose	1 cup/1 tablespoon	4.5 ounces/0.3 ounce	125 grams/8 grams
Flour, whole wheat	1 cup	4 ounces	120 grams
Fruit, dried	1 cup	4 ounces	120 grams
Fruits or veggies, chopped	1 cup	5 to 7 ounces	145 to 200 grams
Fruits or veggies, puréed	1 cup	8.5 ounces	245 grams
Honey, maple syrup, or corn syrup	1 tablespoon	.75 ounce	20 grams
Liquids: cream, milk, water, or juice	1 cup	8 fluid ounces	240 milliliters
Oats	1 cup	5.5 ounces	150 grams
Salt	1 teaspoon	0.2 ounces	6 grams
Spices: cinnamon, cloves, ginger, or nutmeg (ground)	1 teaspoon	0.2 ounce	5 milliliters
Sugar, brown, firmly packed	1 cup	7 ounces	200 grams
Sugar, white	1 cup/1 tablespoon	7 ounces/0.5 ounce	200 grams/12.5 grams
Vanilla extract	1 teaspoon	0.2 ounce	4 grams

OVEN TEMPERATURES

Fahrenheit	Celcius	Gas Mark
225°	110°	$1/4$
250°	120°	$1/2$
275°	140°	1
300°	150°	2
325°	160°	3
350°	180°	4
375°	190°	5
400°	200°	6
425°	220°	7
450°	230°	8